WHEN THE GOING GETS TOUGH

Steve McNally

First Published in Great Britain 2023
by mPowr (Publishing) Limited

www.mpowrpublishing.com

A catalogue record for this book is available from the British Library

ISBN – 978-1-907282-98-0

Design by Alex Casey
Cover by Martyn Pentecost
mPowr Publishing 'Clumpy ™' Logo by e-nimation.com
Clumpy ™ and the Clumpy ™ Logo are trademarks of mPowr Limited

mPowr Publishing Presents...

When you pick up a book by mPowr Publishing you are in for an adventure. Our passion is transformational content, ideas, stories, tools and strategies that empower lives, businesses and communities. You are not likely to get what you expect, but you will find what you need. We don't do bland, generic information. We celebrate the inner quirk, the outer quest and the joy of building legacies that last. Adventurers, Be Enchanted!

Steve McNally

When the Going Gets Tough

A JOURNEY FROM THE STREETS OF NORTHERN IRELAND
TO EFFECTIVE LEADERSHIP IN LIFE AND BUSINESS

To Gillian and my two sons, Ewan and Finn.
This journey could not have happened without you!

Raymond Mulligan—thank you.

Educo World Seminar—thank you for the reset.

Contents

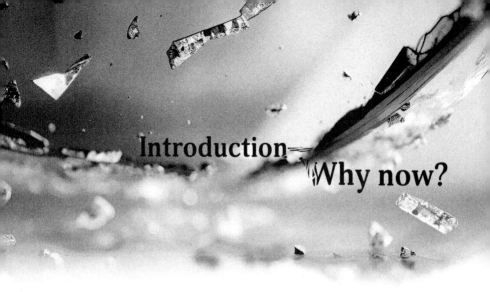

Introduction — Why now?

I have been very fortunate to have found a path in life that has brought me so many wonderful experiences, people, and opportunities. There have been challenges, of course, and that is to be expected, but nothing that I have not been able to deal with, and with each one, I have learnt lessons that I could apply when faced with later obstacles.

Not everyone has the benefit of experience for lots of reasons, but we all can benefit from the stories of the experiences lived by those others who are prepared to share them with generosity and love. Although my starting point in life felt at times like rock bottom, I wasn't stuck there. I want to share my story with you so that you can benefit from my experience. It is imperfectly expressed with generosity and love, and I hope that you find something, however small, that helps you be a better version of yourself, and maybe you can then help someone else do the same.

Ordinarily, six-year-old boys would not be expected to remember much about other people's birthdays, but my sister's fourth birthday will stick with me for the rest of my life. Why? It was 1979, and four days earlier, on 6 March, our father had been blown up by an under-vehicle improvised explosive device (UVIED).

It turns out that Dad's murder was a test run of a type of device, a mercury-switch bomb, which was later used to kill Airey Neave, the then-Conservative Shadow Northern Ireland Secretary. He was assassinated as he was leaving the House of Commons on 30 March, by the same Irish Nationalist Liberation Army (INLA) cell that killed my father. A successful experiment indeed, but it left a little boy in turmoil.

Maybe that incident, happening when I was at such a young age, significantly altered the course of my life. Who would I have been if my father hadn't been murdered and was still around as I was growing up?

Where we start does not need to be where we finish. In the following pages, I am going to share my journey openly and honestly, and as you walk with me, I invite you to reflect on your life and consider the challenges and opportunities that it presents to you. What did life look like for me, and how might you take that and use it—for building a better team, developing a leadership offering, being aware of your environment and mindset, or, at the most fundamental level, considering what it takes to be a modern parent or guardian?

For as long as I can remember, I have sought betterment, challenge, change, and even danger, in buckets. Somehow, I have always come through. Was it because of luck, military training, a deep desire to be the person I needed when I was six years old or a combination of all these factors? Join me as I share my story, and you can decide the answer to those questions. What counts more than anything is how you choose to live your life and what factors you allow to determine your outcomes and the people you enlist to help you.

Although there are references to many people and situations in this book, one must not be forgotten. For nearly thirty years of my life's journey I have had the most important woman next to me. Gillian, my wife, is without doubt my biggest support and supporter. She is an amazing woman, wife, professional teacher, friend, and mother to my two boys as well as being a sister and daughter. I couldn't ask for more.

Before we dive into my story, let me finish this introduction by saying that some of the people who were with me along the way are no longer here, and there's not a day that goes by when I don't think of them. Many of them helped me more than they probably realised, and in doing that—helping this one human being whose words you are reading—they left the world in a better place. I hope that my words and actions help to ensure that I leave the world in a better place as well.

One Bomb, Two Murders

NO ORDINARY TUESDAY

Although 6 March 1979 started as an ordinary day, the events that took place on that Tuesday morning were set to change my life unimaginably and forever. As I sat innocently in a quiet primary school classroom, learning the basics of reading and writing, a loud explosion rocked a neighbourhood in another part of Portadown, the small town where we lived, in County Armagh, Northern Ireland.

Around 1000 hours—that's ten in the morning to civvies and those not as accustomed to the twenty-four-hour clock as people like me who have served in the armed forces—a 26-year-old member of Northern Ireland's Ulster Defence Regiment (UDR) was driving slowly in the car park of the Magowan Buildings.

As the vehicle began to climb a very slight gradient, it tilted just enough for a tiny amount of mercury, housed in a small glass vessel, to roll onto a pair of contacts, closing a circuit and detonating the UVIED that was strapped to the underside of the car near the driving seat.

The force of the explosion ripped through the car, distorting the metal frame, blowing out the glass and doing its very best to separate the flesh from the bones of the driver.

AN EARLY START TO ADULTHOOD

The man behind the wheel had no chance, and the blast took one of his legs, rendering him unconscious. Sadly, he never regained consciousness and on Monday, 13 March, married father of two, Robert McNally, succumbed to his injuries. That man was my father.

3

Seven days earlier, when the bomb was detonated, I was just an ordinary six-year-old boy in a classroom, oblivious to the fallout that was coming my way. When the shockwave hit, it turned my life upside down. The explosion that killed Dad, just three days after my sister's fourth birthday, was responsible for two murders—my father and the wee boy inside me. From that moment, my childhood was over.

AN INDISCRIMINATE KILLER

Explosive devices don't discriminate. Unlike a gun, which must be aimed purposefully at a specific target before the trigger is squeezed, a bomb will cause devastation to anyone and anything in the vicinity. To think that my sister and I had been sat in that car only a few hours earlier sends shivers down my spine even today, over 40 years later. Had the killers who planted the device watched to make sure we'd already been taken to school, or was it sheer luck that the bomb was planted later in the morning? What if we had not gone to school for whatever reason? I often wonder how humanity could stoop so low, what kind of people could carry out such attacks, and what makes this sort of thing legitimate in their eyes.

A BIT OF CONTEXT—THE TROUBLES

For clarity, I will assume that you don't know about the nature and history of the conflict between Britain and Ireland, and I am going to focus on the most recent period of unrest to give some context to the situation I grew up with in the seventies and eighties.

By the beginning of the twentieth century, most people in Ireland wanted to break free of the country's ties with Britain; however, a large chunk of those living in the north of Ireland wanted to remain British, and they launched a campaign to maintain Ireland's union with Great Britain. This led to friction, which is still not resolved even though the region is largely free from terrorist violence, and the community remains divided.

Significant numbers of people on both sides of the argument were prepared to use violence in support of their cause, violence which led to the loss of many lives without ever delivering the solutions the perpetrators had promised the communities who often helped cover their tracks.

OPERATION BANNER

By the 1960s, understandably, frustrations within the Catholic, nationalist community found expression in a campaign for civil rights that drew much of its inspiration from the civil rights marches in the USA. This coincided with the launch of the longest-running operational deployment in British military history. Operation Banner lasted thirty years and marked the start of what has become known as The Troubles, a period that is synonymous with brutality, murder, and hatred and yet also features stories of how the desire for unity overcame the divisions of nationalism and loyalism, exemplifying humanity at its best.

The Troubles caused the death of 3,500 people, including my father. Thousands more were injured, and thousands more were traumatised by violence; however, by the 1990s, there was recognition that violence would not deliver a solution to the conflict and that any effort to find a political answer would only succeed if republican and loyalist paramilitaries were given a voice at the negotiating table.

A DIVIDED COMMUNITY

That table, led by our politicians today, remains divided and unable to govern free from the shackles of our history, which means that although free from the levels of violence once seen, we are not moving forward as one community.

Around the time when my father was murdered, we were living in an area of Portadown that was on the front line of the conflict, and I believe that bomb was the final straw of a bit of a haystack. One of my earliest memories is of being banned from playing with my friend Shaun.

Shaun was Catholic, I was Protestant, and our innocence was irrelevant. When I was told that I wasn't allowed to play with him anymore, I couldn't understand, and it hurt me deeply. Sadly, it didn't take long for me to realise that the end of our friendship was only the beginning, and many other restrictions would follow that had nothing to do with me or my beliefs and values—symptoms of the times we were living in.

A DOWNWARD SPIRAL

Very shortly after being banned from spending time with Shaun, our dog was taken and killed. It was becoming increasingly clear that we were no longer wanted in the area as the demographic continued to change at a raging pace. The situation continued to escalate, taking a more sinister and targeted turn when a hoax bomb was placed at the front door of our house. I vividly remember being taken out of the house in a blanket by my uncle and moved to a safe location while the Army dealt with the incident. Little did I or anyone else apart from the perpetrators know that this was part of a wider plan to monitor the Army's bomb alert response times and procedures.

Although it was very difficult for a six-year-old to understand what was happening around us, I was well aware that we were not safe anymore; but what could I do about it—I was just a wee boy. My mum understood what was happening and moved us out of the family home when she could see the direction things were going. From antisocial behaviour to killing the family pet to bringing the bomb squad to our home—what next?

WRONG PLACE, WRONG TIME

My father was defiant, but he was a soldier after all, and he may have unwittingly caused some of the attention we were getting by being less than discreet when coming to and from our home. I later discovered that not only was Dad indiscreet, but he actively antagonised the local members of the paramilitary group, the INLA—the same people who went on to plant the car bomb that killed him.

That bomb, a switch UVIED, used what has become known as a mercury-tilt switch as a fuse. All it takes is the slightest vibration, and a small amount of mercury will connect the two contacts in a circuit, and the UVIED will detonate. The INLA was carrying out a test run of the device when they killed Dad, who happened to be a convenient target right on the organisation's doorstep. The person they were most interested in assassinating was Airey Neave, the then-British Shadow Secretary of State for Northern Ireland.

On 30 March 1979, a cell of INLA members used the same kind of mercury-tilt switch UVIED to murder Neave, by fixing the device in the exact position on his car as they had done to my father's vehicle—on the underside of the car, near to the driver's seat. He died shortly after being admitted to hospital.

FLASHPOINT MEMORIES

The day I found out that my father was dead, I was sitting in the chair at the window in the corner of the living room of our new home, a flat in another part of Portadown. I liked sitting there because it gave me a cracking view of the park and the trees that I would come to love climbing in and, bizarrely, collecting snails from. We were still settling in, so I didn't know anyone and wasn't sure why we were there or why we had not seen Dad for eight days. Those questions were about to be answered!

Mum came into the room, and my sister joined me in the corner seat, and that's when she explained what had been going on and why we hadn't seen Dad for so long. Then she shared the horrible news that our father was dead, and we would never be able to see him again. I don't recall her exact words. Maybe I blocked them out. What I do remember, which may seem hard to believe or strange to others, is the overwhelming feeling of unfairness that this had happened to me, my family, and my father.

When we experience intensely traumatic or shocking moments, sometimes we block out the most painful bits to protect ourselves, but what's left remains etched in our minds forever as flashbulb memories. The flashbulb memory created by the news of Dad's murder was powerful and big enough to envelop mundane events from the week before and after, including my sister's fourth birthday.

Everything about that day is as raw now as it was then, but you may be shocked to learn that the trauma for me was not so much about finding out my father was dead; that didn't come as a surprise, and I even half-knew that was going to happen.

Over the years, perhaps since that moment, I have honed an instinct for situational awareness, often visualising what is coming next just before it does. Perhaps, subconsciously, I had already developed some skill in that area and was absorbing the atmosphere of Portadown without consciously understanding what the fuss was about. Intuitively, I could sense meaning from the world around me.

MAN OF THE HOUSE

The news that Mum imparted to me that day was absorbed and processed, at least superficially, and I moved on emotionally very quickly. Losing a parent at such a young age leaves a massive hole that the person who is left behind may not be aware of until adulthood, if ever—the sense of abandonment and the loss of the person they looked up to for guidance, to name a couple of big issues; however, there were more practical consequences that I knew I would have to adapt to.

Dad's death marked the abrupt end of my childhood and the death of the wee boy inside me. I vowed to be the man of our house and to protect my sister, something which I failed to achieve on several occasions and struggled to forgive myself for in the decades that followed. I'm going to revisit forgiveness later.

There are two school years between me and my sister, and this meant that I was always close to keep an eye on her when she needed me or even when she didn't know she needed me. This dynamic continued and went on to form the spine of our relationship for years to come.

Mum appeared to move on from the murder of her husband as quickly as I moved on from the death of my father, but I cannot know for sure. It's the conclusion I came to, based on the fact that, once we had been told about his murder, the topic was never discussed again. So what? Not talking about stuff is something that has developed into a recurring theme in our family, and that has left many unsaid words and allowed gaps to grow in the grieving process, especially for my sister, Cheryl. Only the other day, when I was talking to her about this part of the book, she said, 'I wonder what he would think of me now,' with a tear welling up in her eye—over 40 years since he passed away.

Cheryl has her own business and three lovely children but has, at times, been unhappy with how her life has turned out. I can't help but think that if we had spoken more about our father, and if my mum had stepped up and been emotionally courageous enough to talk about him in a child-appropriate manner and lay on me and Cheryl with the kind of affirmations that a father might lay on his children, we would know what he would have thought of us; not for sure objectively, of course, but we would have felt certain because the programming would have convinced us of it. In the grand scheme of things, feelings are sometimes more valuable than facts, especially for young minds when they are developing.

PEELING THE ONION

Much remains unsaid in our immediate family but not for long; peeling this onion is at the top of my hit list. I am fortunate that my sister and I have a close relationship and can talk about the challenges we shared as children. I continue to be her big brother which, second only to being a loving husband and father, is my most treasured role. For many others in my family, there is a wall of silence.

We moved home again shortly after the news of Dad's murder, to a house that was in very poor condition and felt grubby and dirty. I could not understand why we had moved so soon and, of course, did not get a reason; however, the place was soon looking spic and span and, actually, the cul-de-sac we moved to was great, full of kids of our age, and we quickly settled into what felt like a very safe place to be. We were not alone for long, though.

8

A NEW MAN OF THE HOUSE

A new man arrived in the house, and he was there to stay. This didn't sit well with me as I was the self-declared man of the house, and I immediately threw myself into a battle for power. I was eight. Who did I think I was? I knew who I was, and I was determined to play my role, which often meant being a bit disruptive as this new man, who shall remain nameless as there was an incident that makes naming him difficult, issued instructions in the house.

Mostly, it was his presence that annoyed me, so he didn't have to do anything to earn my wrath, and he didn't appear to be a bad person. Sometimes, I allowed myself, the little tyrant, to enjoy his company. After all, he had become almost as much a part of our life as Dad.

Time is a funny thing, and how we experience it is entirely subjective. It bends and distorts. We didn't have long with our father, six good years, but because we were so young, it felt like a fleeting moment and very few memories exist. Meanwhile, time was passing slowly with our new lodger, and he'd soon been with us for as long as my sister had been alive when our father was murdered. Time with Dad was shrinking all the time as a memory, while time with the house guest was steadily lengthening. We were used to him.

Almost as violently as our father's death, the new man was gone! *What had happened?* Given the lack of talking that I've already spelt out, we got a very paltry, 'He's gone.' Even though it turns out there was a long list of reasons for him to be gone, we did not get to hear any of them at the time. Of course, I thought I had got rid of him, that my mission to oust him was accomplished, so I was clear to reclaim my man-of-the-house role again—and legitimately, as I was always there when the other men who showed up were not.

Our childhood was full of fun and laughter despite what was happening around us in our house. We had lots of friends, I had discovered the joy of BMX riding, and I was not far from my grandmother's house. I was very close to Gran and used to enjoy hanging around with her in the garden, which was full, from hedge to hedge, with the vegetables and soft fruits that she grew every season, even in not-so-sunny Northern Ireland.

All was well for a while until my man-of-the-house role looked likely to become threatened again, or so I thought. New man, same offer—nothing. I was eleven by this stage and a pretty forceful young kid, and I made him know how I felt and never let up. To his credit, he stayed and married my mum, so I had, in title only, a stepdad—but not in spirit, and I never once acknowledged his place in my life. This was partly due to his weakness as a man, based on my perception of what I thought it would take to be a good dad. Of course, this was based on my imagination, images of heroes that I was watching on TV, the likes of Steve Austin in *The Six Million Dollar Man* and Colt Seavers in *The Fall Guy*, both played by Lee Majors. Funny, now that I think about it, but I have continued to model my behaviours as a dad on those early perceptions that I conjured up—I do not run in slow motion like Steve or jump from a tall building like Colt, but I set high standards for myself as a dad.

The new imposter failed to impress me in any way, and the situation was made even worse when we moved again to where he was from. Another grubby house and miles from my school and friends; I was pretty pissed off it was fair to say. I didn't move school and stubbornly went about building my own life as the one that was being built for me did not appeal. By then, I was thirteen, and I was moving on and paving my own way.

LOOKING FOR AN EXIT

Northern Ireland was still very divided and I, like that little boy who did not understand why he could not play with Shaun, was not happy with being labelled as one or the other in the religious mayhem that still defined the streets where we lived and played. At fourteen, I decided that I was not going to live my life with this choice and made a commitment to leave Northern Ireland at the earliest opportunity.

There was not a lot of prosperity in Northern Ireland at the time and coming from my extremely working-class, sometimes not even working background, the escape route did not look too easy. One newspaper article jumped out at me—Army Careers. That was it, my mind was made up, and everything I did from that moment was gearing me towards joining the Army at eighteen years old.

I would not be confined or defined by the situation in Northern Ireland. I would set my own path.

In one moment, because of one advertisement, a fuse within my heart detonated, an explosion followed, and I was set free. The goal was set. All that remained was the execution. I got a part-time job, did what I needed to at school (just about), and prepared for life in the British Army.

As I write, it is 27 October 2022 and, quite fortuitously, today marks the launch of the Royal British Legion Poppy Appeal and the start of my journey to commit my thoughts to words on a page.

My whole life has been influenced by the military, legitimately as a serving officer, and illegitimately as a victim of The Troubles in Northern Ireland, like so many others. My father was a soldier, my grandfather was a veteran of World War Two, and growing up in Northern Ireland in the 1970s meant violence and conflict were never too far away. Perhaps, I was destined to become a soldier.

In this chapter, I have given you some glimpses of my childhood and the world I grew up in. Over the course of this book, I am going to show you how those experiences have helped me adapt and grow in later life, but the timeline will not be linear.

I will try to balance academic insight with my experience to help articulate the message so that it is not all hot air and history, and I hope you find what I share useful personally, for a friend or family member, or even for someone in your work or business life.

Some of my experiences have been challenging, some plastered with extreme violence, some funny, some very special, and some deeply sad. All of them have helped build a better version of me, a version that I could never have hoped for, given the start I had and nearly didn't have considering the circumstances on that fateful morning of 6 March 1979 when I could have been in that car when the bomb exploded.

We have all been programmed by our upbringing to some degree. Like other biases such as racism, we are not born with these shackles, and we can, with acknowledgement and work, shake them off.

Don't let your own biggest enemy live between your two ears.

Laird Hamilton, Big Wave Surfer

When the going gets tough, what do the tough do?

Strap yourself in, and I will help you find the answer or at least give you some tools to kick the journey off. Remember that a march of a thousand miles starts with the first step. This chapter was your first step. Now, it's time for the next.

Searching for Dad

Losing my father so violently, both in how he was killed and its suddenness, left me with a huge hole to fill. Fathers are to young boys as satnavs are to those navigating a route to somewhere they've never been. Children can feel lost without their parents and boys look to their fathers for guidance. I've had a lifetime to consider how the death of my father impacted me and, in this chapter, I am going to introduce, explore, and share some of the main themes relating to fathers, sons, and father-son relationships.

It's funny how often we do things without knowing we are doing them. When I lost my father, I immediately felt that I had a responsibility to fill his shoes. What a load of bollocks! I was barely out of short trousers, so who did I think I was? And that's the point: At that age, I didn't know who I was. I didn't have enough time under my belt to have a meaningful sense of who I was and as a young boy, I wanted—no, needed—a father to show me. Given my determination to be the man of the house, the sooner I could get that guidance the better. I needed it desperately.

A deep emotional connection to experiences and stories is our best learning medium. Who would be there to let me make the mistakes that would enrich me as I matured? Who would curate the stories that would shape me? Under whose watchful eye was my journey to unfold?

PSYCHOLOGICAL LITERACY

Of course, I am no longer so naive as to think that is the way all father-son relationships turn out. It is, however, not too unrealistic to want a role model, someone who loves us unconditionally but will guide us even when it means chastising and correcting poor behaviour. This is as relevant now as it has ever been. Today, we understand the needs more than ever with the abundance of information available to us; indeed, you could argue that we all should be able to achieve psychological literacy on a personal level on our own.

Psychological literacy is, in its most basic form, an understanding of how to be insightful and reflective about not only one's own behaviours and mental processes but that of others. It's easy to see how this is relevant to the context of a boy learning how to be a man through the guidance of their father and in many ways, this is a tried and tested formula. We need only to look to the animal kingdom, be it the art of the hunt or even survival from predators or just in good old figuring out how to be.

While I knew that I yearned for a father figure, I was very much getting on with being me. On reflection, I did not legitimise instruction from the adults around me at home, including my mother or any of the men who became part of our family unit, not because I was not able or willing to but simply because they did not make the quality line that I had set. Outrageous when you think of my age and position in the family unit at that stage in my life, but apart from my sports coaches or the teachers who I believed set good examples of what it was to be a strong male, I pretty much ignored every other adult.

Now I understand that I empowered myself unless I empowered others by deeming them worthy enough to be considered as any kind of mentor, guide, or role model. This was a risky strategy as the checks and balances had constraints. Those whom I empowered had little time to create and deepen influence, and they did not know I had charged them with this responsibility, so any failings on their part would be spotted and magnified by me without them knowing how important their behaviour was. Even if they had been aware, the only opportunity they had to lead was while I was with them in the classroom or on the rugby pitch. The rest of the time, I was a law unto myself, 'leading the self'.

MEN IN THE HOME

The men/potential fathers who came in and out of my and my mother's family life, even the one who hung around the longest but (to be fair) added the least value considering the timescale, were, unbeknownst to me, building my subliminal understanding of psychological literacy.

Some theories say that to be truly psychologically literate, there are nine attributes we need to have and display. As well as being insightful and reflective, being psychologically literate includes:

- Psychological knowledge—the state of being familiar with something or aware of its existence, usually resulting from experience or academic study. My understanding, certainly the knowledge I am sharing within this book, is from experience.
- Scientific thinking—a type of knowledge seeking that involves intentional information gathering, including asking questions, testing hypotheses, making observations and collaborating with evidence. In today's world, data is key, and you will often hear the call for data-based decision-making.
- Critical thinking—the intellectually disciplined process of actively and skilfully conceptualising, applying, analysing and evaluating information gathered pre decision-making or planning.
- Application of psychological principles—applied psychology is the application of psychological principles to solve problems of the human experience and can be applied anywhere from the workplace to the battlefield.
- Ethical behaviour—ethical behaviour is what guides us to do the right thing, tell the truth or simply do no harm and help when we can. This has scope to be manipulated depending on our beliefs; my measure is about how my ethics help me make decisions that create positive impacts and importantly avoid unjust or negative impacts. This is the tricky one on the list for sure.
- Information literacy—This is particularly important for those who have the power to make decisions, especially if they are on behalf of others. It is the ability to find, evaluate, organise and use information in all its formats to make good, informed decisions. In my military career, this was very important as the result of a bad decision could mean the loss of life. Information is king!
- Effective communication skills—This is the simplest aspect of psychological literacy to understand but can be the most difficult to achieve, especially if, like me, you have had to socially mobilise yourself, had an education that is less than perfect or culturally you are not confident in expressing yourself; all of that is before we add in the additional challenges of introversion or neurodiversity.
- Respect for diversity, equality, and inclusion—This is not

just having respect and acceptance but actively seeking out diversity across its many considerations, not just the obvious gender or race, offering equity, not just equality, and being inclusive in a manner that gives everyone a voice.

We are all aware of these principles to some degree, and I am sure we can all recognise some of these in ourselves and indeed could admit to needing to work on some or all of them on some level. Not so for a wee boy, however, who was lost in who to be and how to be it. Although I was values-driven from an early age, I wasn't self-aware enough to know it.

At a time when I was trying to learn how to be and who I wanted to be, from the age of seven to fourteen, the only models of masculinity I had in the home were poor. What other competencies would I need to acquire to break clear of their terrible examples of behaviours, lack of courage, poverty syndrome and downright laziness? When I say laziness, I don't just mean that in its simplest form. I am talking about not taking steps to be better by refusing to accept where we are and striving to reach where we could be—the cycle of attracting the minimum and blaming the environment for it.

Learning to be is one of four pillars of a structure first outlined in a report called *The Treasure Within*, which was submitted to the United Nations Educational, Scientific and Cultural Organization (UNESCO) by the then-chairman of the International Commission on Education for the Twenty-first Century, Jacques Delors. It is a system I have used over the last few years to promote a change in approach to how we train young people coming into the world of work, specifically within the field of professional services, which is where I find myself now. This is work that I have been fortunate to have won recognition and awards for, but, boy, do I wish I knew then what I know now, back when that wee boy needed to know how to make sense of what was happening to him. Well, it's never too late!

The other three pillars are learning to be together, learning to know, and learning to do. For now, I'd like to focus on learning to be, and the part that played in helping to shape me into the person I am today.

LEARNING TO BE

While I searched for a father in my early years, I didn't realise that what I was actually searching for was psychological literacy. I didn't need a person, but if I were going to benefit from having someone to guide me, their persona would have to reflect mine. What I needed was simple—an example of my values and an opportunity to be guided on my path to learning to be.

Faith, while not a theme of this book, is something that we all can benefit from, regardless of what each of us uniquely believes. I became aware of something greater than myself at the age of around ten and took myself off to a place of worship for me to explore. My relationship with a higher power is something I have never quite mastered even as I try a new place of worship today, but what I do believe is that the connection I feel is real and the values are close to my heart. Perhaps, this is where my father has always been—there, right in front of me—but like many a child, I have denied its presence and therefore missed out on the benefit of its stewardship and love.

Although I missed many opportunities, either because I didn't recognise them or indeed because I ignored them, thinking I knew better, I am truly grateful for one that didn't escape me when I was a teenager. It was a chance that arose spontaneously and not by design, at least not by my design, when, at the age of around fourteen, I got a part-time job in a fish-and-chip shop. It was not a glamorous opportunity by a long shot but one that I grabbed with the enthusiasm of an Olympic athlete accepting a gold medal.

What unfolded over the next four years that I worked there is the story of how I truly learnt to be. Like any learning journey, the enabling conditions are critical to success, and if we are ever to achieve transformational learning or change in a cultural growth or transformational programme, the conditions must first be right, not perfect. The world is and always has been complex, and technology seems to be moving at its fastest pace every new day. There have been many technological revolutions, but the digital transformation that the world is experiencing today is perhaps one of the most fast-moving and omnipresent ever.

Learning to be is not just a personal journey, but it is also about acquiring the competencies needed to succeed. For the benefit of this book, I am defining competence as *the ability to meet challenges in any environment in a complex landscape*. For any individual to achieve that means learning through the experiences of engaging with complex challenges that not only motivate them but also benefit the wider stakeholder community. Working in the chip shop was about to become my most enriched learning environment to date on many levels.

A VERSION OF DAD—KEITH

If I thought my search was about finding a father, I had achieved the mission, at least as far as finding a male mentor who I looked up to and who reflected my values in everything that he did was concerned.

I was instantly drawn to Keith, the owner of the fish shop, but he was not so drawn to me at the beginning! He did not want teenagers on his staff and although he agreed to give me a chance, this was with the expectation that I would probably fail to impress. Little did he know that once given the chance to do something that I wanted, I would be like the dog that refuses to let go of the bone, and he had no idea what I was capable of.

Keith was an exceptionally hard-working man and although it was only a small, local fish-and-chip shop, he had introduced lots of innovation that I don't think he fully appreciated but I did. I delivered on every level and sought to exceed expectations. When he asked me to do one thing, I did two; when he set a standard, I went a step further; when there was space in the rhythm of the customer flow, I looked for an opportunity to improve things, doing small tasks such as cleaning machines that were already clean by most people's standards but not mine. I set high standards, and he kept giving me the space to grow. Keith trusted me with something dear—his business and customers.

I shadowed him, but he didn't know I was doing it or at least he didn't show it, and I observed everything he did, keen to demonstrate continuous growth in my competency and to show that I should be trusted to take on other responsibilities.

In a very short time, I was working 32 hours a week in the shop, which was unusual for a fourteen-year-old, but I can now see that it was as destructive as it was productive. Why? My time should have been more evenly balanced between friends, socialising, and simply being a child. Although I was highly capable, I wasn't spending enough time in school because I was poorly motivated by its academic offering, and being with the family unit was the last place I wanted to be.

LEAVING HOME

Home is the place where I should have been guided, and I think Mum could have and should have intervened to help me gain more balance. It was not to be, and I would have been difficult to persuade anyway. Keith could have done it, but why would he when he had an increasingly competent right-hand person to help him run his business? That is where Mum could have applied pressure without me even knowing, but, alas, she offered no guidance, no advice, no interest or even recognition of the need of a fourteen-year-old to be guided and nurtured through the difficult teenage years.

If I am going to be brutally honest about it, I may as well have left home at fourteen because mentally, I had entered the world of adulthood and independence under the stewardship of my boss, even though I was still sleeping at the family home. Keith provided me with an example of what the rewards of hard work can bring, he gave me the opportunity and trust to push myself, and he gave me rewards for succeeding in the form of affirmation and financial bonuses.

In later years, Keith told me that he never had an employee that matched what I brought and that I had helped him be a better version of himself when he was working with me. That is the most powerful piece of professional feedback I have ever had, and it came in response to the efforts of a wee boy between the age of fourteen to eighteen. Words endure history, so be careful with yours!

Keith is one of the few people in this book whom I have not anonymised as he has had such a lasting and transformational impact on my life, I wanted to celebrate him, and also because there are no security issues attached to being open about him as there are for some of the other individuals I will be mentioning.

SEARCHING FOR MYSELF

In Keith, I found a version of what I believed a father should look like, but what I have subsequently learnt is that I was not searching for a father per se; I was searching for myself and have been all of my life, and I hope that this has made me a reflective practitioner, to use the phrase coined by Donald Schön.

Schön observed that the rapidly changing nature of the challenges posed in our modern world requires us to develop beyond just technical expertise, and in doing so, we become problem solvers—not just in the traditional sense but by taking a problem-setting approach, i.e., falling in love with the problem, not the solution, so that we bring about right result over the right method. Reflective practice means looking critically at how challenges are approached and being open-minded enough to adapt as more is learnt about the problems being dealt with.

Searching for Dad has led me not to a father figure but to myself. Reflecting, I now fully appreciate that I was looking for someone to put my trust in to develop me and put me on the right path, and that person turns out to be me. This does not, by any means, diminish the opportunity that is presented by having a father who does all the things I was hoping for from the father I was yearning for from the age of six—imagine what I might have become if I had that father from the outset. I have come to appreciate that knowing ourselves is fundamental if we are to grow continually, physically, and mentally, throughout this journey we call life.

THE IMPORTANCE OF SELF-AWARENESS

Emotional self-awareness is so important that I believe it to be the foundation on which most of the other elements that make up emotional intelligence (EQ) are built. Developing this is surely the first step towards exploring yourself and coming to understand how you work and how you might work with others.

Two of the biggest challenges in gaining a higher level of emotional self-awareness are recognition and admission. You can't manage what you don't recognise, and you won't manage what you don't admit.

In my early life, I thought I had been robbed of a father who had all the answers to my endless questions, and I managed that situation badly in that I took it upon myself to either sort or rebel against the machine. I imagine that was not easy for those around me, and I was probably quite a difficult child to manage. What I needed was a guide and they were always available to me, but I was so narrow-minded that I thought a father was the only manifestation available to me, and I fell in love with the solution, not the problem. Had I taken Schön's approach, I would have recognised what the real problem was.

A lack of self-awareness will cloud your ability to recognise what you're doing, why you are doing it, and how it may be affecting others who are close to you either in the workplace or home. You will not be capable of changing if your blinkered view is preventing you from seeing the truth, and you will be stuck with the sad view that there's nothing wrong so no need to change. We see this in so many transactional leaders who have power by authority and not necessarily approval.

Self-awareness is arguably the most essential element of EQ, a quality that can help us achieve more than we could through the science of management and process alone. Managing this one overarching skill to a point where you are unconsciously competent will empower you to work towards improvement in all areas of EQ and is indeed likely to drive cohesion and performance in your work and home life. Without this ingredient though, you are likely to continue the merry-go-round of fixing the same problems repeatedly. Using that approach, you will fail to get valuable feedback, the food of improvement and a privilege if sought early and implemented at the first opportunity. I must add that feedback should never be used to cause hurt or offence; if it is used to deliver either of these things, it will very quickly be left in the wilderness, and everyone suffers as a result.

A DISEMPOWERED MOTHER

When I think of my time working in the chippy, blissfully tuned into every word and action of Keith, and ignoring everything else around me, I wonder what I missed or, more importantly, what impact this had on my mother. Now, I can see how my behaviours of growing independence both physically and financially could have been hurtful. I was earning a considerable wage per week and could buy everything I needed with my own money. I thought this was reducing the financial pressure in the house, but it was quite possibly difficult for my mother to witness my apparent rejection of her as my primary caregiver and Mum.

By that time, we had a new baby in the house, Haley, but I didn't have a lot of time to invest in her and behaved more like a lodger than a son or a brother. There were things that I wanted, which I would have liked to have found at 38 Festival Road but weren't there, especially regarding relationships. Unconsciously, I probably denied everyone the opportunity to be better or to even understand what I needed and wasn't getting—everyone, that is, apart from my eldest sister. I have always felt a sense of responsibility toward her as a big brother and wanted to be there to provide the support that a father might otherwise offer. She, like me, was not given the stability or, at least, the hope of a traditional two-point-four upbringing.

TRIGGERS

From the day my father died, I was never able to use the word *Dad* when I was growing up because it was triggering, and that created a very strong aversion to talking about what people were doing other than what I could see or was participating in. Anyone skilled in the art of communication and truly empathising with how I felt will realise that such an aversion meant that my topics of conversation were significantly curtailed.

Have you ever watched television shows such as *Breaking Dad* where Barney Walsh pushes his father, Bradley Walsh, to experience extreme situations and has a ball doing it while their already visibly beautiful father and son relationship blossoms even more? Or Jack Whitehall's *Travels with My Father*, which taps into a similar theme? I have, and it is one of my ouch points—I feel angry that although there was never any guarantee that that is how my relationship with my father would have turned out, it might have! This anger is something that has caused me some issues over the years and is definitely one of my EQ devils, and although I am aware of it, I have not always been able to manage it. I have since learnt that my anger is a symptom, not the disease, and it is natural, especially in the face of loss, either real or perceived.

I have strived, especially over the last ten years, to be conscious of my anger and why I might be feeling that way. This has certainly helped prevent me from being driven mad by internal forces that have in the past pushed me into self-defeating behaviours, which have seen me seek out and/or perpetrate violence.

In dealing with my anger demons, I have acknowledged my ouch points, tried to remove myself from the environments that might add to the internal talk that can lead to anger, utilised a framework or method that calms me down and shifts maladaptive self-talk to a more realistic inner monologue that wrestles back control. It is my Doc Banner versus Hulk or Jackal and Hyde conflict.

Much of my anger stemmed from not having a relationship with my father, but instead of dwelling on the relationship I couldn't have, I should have been focusing on the relationships I did. I have also learnt to acknowledge that the circumstances that led to this were not my doing and totally out of my control, and this has helped a lot, but I am still a work in progress.

THE SEARCH IS OVER

My search for Dad took me to many different places—Keith, friends that I have been attracted to over the years who are older than me but share my values and whom I look up to for the example that they have set, the Army metaphorically as it is built on relationships that depend on each other delivering on a contracted basis and is very values-driven, and faith in a Christian God.

None of these searches delivered what I was looking for, but I now recognise that I was searching for the wrong thing, so of course they didn't deliver what I needed. What I needed was time and awareness of how to flourish as my authentic self. If it is to be, it is up to me, has become a motto that I return to often when

considering a challenge or a change I want to face or introduce.

The search for Dad is over. The exercise brought many answers, even revelations, but there are still questions to be answered; only now, the answers or absence of answers will not define me. There is still work to be done for me in living up to the imaginary representation of Dad conjured up by that little six-year-old boy when he decided that since Dad was not around, he had to step into the role. If that Dad could have left a message for me, he would almost certainly have said, 'Stand down, Son. There is a path defined for you. Take your time and walk it, and all will be given to you. Be in the present, a child, a brother, a friend, a son, a husband, and a dad when the role calls for you and be your best when you get there.'

Would you believe me if I told you that until today, I had never written a poem in my life? As I reflected on my father and what I believe he would have said to me, this poem spontaneously erupted from my deep core.

STAND DOWN, SON

Be a boy
The man can wait
Ride your bike
Be free, fly, fall, scrape
I've got you, Son, get back up

Live the life that I gave up
Run with me
Laugh with me
Cry with me
Leave the tough stuff with me
Trust me, Son, I am here

When it's dark, know there is light
When there is light, know that I provide
When it's time, take your place
When the call comes, be the one
Carry the light, Son
Carry the light for everyone

Do not sacrifice what you have not yet earned
Your journey must be learnt
Your time precious
The bumps, the bangs, the celebrations
The contributions, affirmations, the confirmations
Just a wee boy who will become a great man

I have lived, loved, and lost
So that you can be found
Live the life that I would have designed for you
Stand down, Son
Stand down, Son
The man can wait

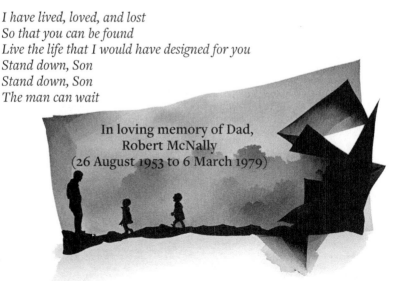

In loving memory of Dad,
Robert McNally
(26 August 1953 to 6 March 1979)

Perhaps it is because of the therapeutic effect of writing this memoir. Either way, these words capture exactly what I believe my father would have said to me and what I would like to say to my son.

But he couldn't leave that message, and it took that wee boy many years to figure things out. The urge to find a new father was only one of the consequences of losing Dad. Knowing how to say goodbye to my original father was another.

Burying Dad

The putrid smell of burnt flesh and the sense of disorientation in that smoke-filled car must have been a nightmare. Except that it wasn't something imagined from a REM-sleep state but the reality of what my father was experiencing on 6 March.

FINAL MOMENTS

What was going through his mind? Is it even possible that he was thinking of anything as he slipped in and out of consciousness? A powerful bomb had exploded just inches from his body and the metal forming the base of his car, far from shielding him from the blast, had been turned into shrapnel, causing him life-changing injuries to his lower limbs. Even if he had been conscious for long enough, he would not have been able to get out of the vehicle, so there was no escaping the burning wreckage until the emergency services arrived. Portadown was a hot spot during The Troubles, so it was not too long before the security forces were on the scene along with an ambulance that took him away to the hospital where he later died of his injuries.

I often wonder how he felt about becoming a father. What were his first thoughts on the day I was born? And I wonder whether he thought about us during his last moments of consciousness before he passed out forever. My instinct tells me that these and many other thoughts about pure survival would have been amplified during those last few moments. He was a soldier and if my experiences are anything to go by, there would have been some anger in there as well—at being the victim, at being robbed of his life as he knew it (and seven days later, life itself), and undoubtedly anger towards his murderers.

AN UNFILLABLE HOLE

My father died on 13 March 1979 and on that day, my sister and I lost something that we hadn't had long enough to even understand where to look or what to look for to fill the hole that was left—what do dads do? Who were we going to make proud? Who was going to be our North Star?

Even at that tender age, I felt a loss that was so deep, it never really got out; I was and still am (self-proclaimed) an alpha male, by which I mean someone who embraces the traditional values of masculinity (protective, action-orientated, etc.), not the toxically male club-yielding caveman the term has come to represent. My very happy home is very traditional in outlook in that I, with validation from my beautiful, funny, smart, and successful wife, hold the head of the household role—a responsibility that I treat very seriously. Being Dad for me and us as a family is very much about protection, provision and being there for everyone, especially if we are facing problems or challenges.

HEADS, YOU LOSE. TAILS, I WIN

I didn't get to find out how my father would have treated the role of dad, except for how he was when I was a wee boy, but I very quickly knew what I would have wanted him to be like. This vision, which I held from such an early age, was both a gift and a poison chalice as I would baseline every man who came into our lives on it. They never stood a chance, and I am sure that the situation I am describing is not unusual with many stepfathers walking into what often starts as a hostile environment for them and many families failing to make it past that first hurdle. Some do, but I never gave any of my mother's potential suitors a chance; the bar was too high and if they got close, I would raise it higher. Heads, you lose. Tails, I win. You may wonder whether I was testing them. Was there a point at which I would surrender and accept them? I doubt it.

A BURIED HOPE

When I buried Dad, physically and metaphorically, I buried all hope of ever having a relationship that could match my vision or expectation; and if we were to look at this through the lens of the Law of Attraction, I ensured it could never happen.

While burying that hope may have instinctively felt like the right thing to do as a natural protection mechanism—against the possibility of being abandoned again (even though my father's exit was not his fault)—it added to my struggle.

In the years that followed, I shied away from conversations about what my friends had done with their fathers. They were too painful. I didn't want to go there because I was so hungry for a story of my own. What could I add to such discussions? I wanted to be able to say that my father had watched me play rugby and taken me for fish and chips afterwards or share similar experiences, but those stories had been stolen from me.

A MAJOR REVELATION

Imagine my surprise when my best friend's mother, while royally pissed (she had alcohol issues), blurted out that I was related to my best friend. I could not work this out and, of course, being the curious young eleven-year-old lad that I was, I immediately began probing my Mum's friend further but with no joy. It seems that Dutch courage or drunk stupidity does know some boundaries, and I think that even though her judgement was impaired, she realised that she had overstepped the moral line.

I was confused and angry, and I wanted answers, so I took my questions to my mother. Remember, I was just a child who was desperately missing a father in ways that I could not articulate at the time. Armed with the new information provided unceremoniously by her piss-head mate, I marched up to my mother and confronted her:

'How am I related to Kevin, Mum?'

Saying you could cut the atmosphere with a knife doesn't come close.

'Son, your daddy was not your real dad. I am sorry. He adopted you, Stephen.'

Hearing those words caused deep pain, which I can still feel today if I choose to. If you have ever been on a mortar base plate or beside a main battle tank when it fires an explosive round, you will know that the air around you gets sucked in like a vacuum, the noise is shattering, and you feel the thunderous bang as though Thor himself has dropped in. Even though it would be a long time before I got to experience that feeling for real, that's exactly how it felt on that summer's day as I heard from my own mother's lips that the man who I had always believed to be my father was not related to me in any way. He was not my biological father.

My heart sank, my lungs felt heavy, and my head was spinning, unable to process what it had just heard. To this day, I am not sure whether I am more annoyed about how I found out or the fact that, for a value-driven person like me, what I had learnt had ripped my very existence apart. Despite everything, I had always believed I was my father's son and in an instant, not even that was true. Everything that I identified with was gone in a sentence.

AFTERMATH

That I was adopted was not as much of an issue as finding out that Robert McNally was not my father—knowing that killed a small part of me there and then. It was as though I had been dragged into a lie without giving my consent, and from that moment, I felt as though every time I referred to him as my dad, I was perpetuating that lie. I was not emotionally intelligent enough to process this, and in typical Steve McNally fashion, I shut it down, never speaking about it again and trying to avoid conversations about my father (or him not being my father, as I felt was the case then, even though he adopted me) until now—in this book.

With the right parental guidance and support, I could easily have dropped any other reality for the one that was defined in law and stated on my adoption certificate, but alas, I was left to deal with it myself, and the unpleasant mix of confusion, pain, and injustice of it all was allowed to fester in my heart and mind. Here we are, almost 40 years on, and that boil has still not been completely lanced.

I felt ashamed, which is not something that any child should feel, especially about something they had no part to play in. Ashamed not only because I believed I had lost the legitimacy of calling Robert my father but because that meant that to do so would be effectively lying. That was when I stopped using the word *Dad*.

As if that was not enough, I was left without the only remaining traces of Robert McNally that I had in my mind—the illusion of a dad. The whole idea was gone. Everything. Worse still, I was old enough to work out that I had been born out of wedlock; it is not such an issue in modern society, but in Ireland in the early seventies, north or south of the border, that got you the title of bastard.

IDENTITY CRISIS

For six years, I had been learning to be *Steve, the young boy who had lost his dad to a terrible act of terrorism*. In an instant, that identity was shattered, and I had to learn to be *Steve, the young boy who lost his adopted dad to a terrible act of terrorism*. I was not sure what was worse—the murder of the person I'd always called Dad or the murder of my memories and identity—and on top of that, I was feeling the loss of that human being who had meant so much to me but had been brutally taken away from me. What remained was a desperate feeling of grief that I neither understood nor was equipped to deal with.

My world had been turned upside down, and I was struggling on every conceivable front to understand why I was here, how I was going to be free of the shame, and most importantly, who was going to help me do that.

LEARNING TO KNOW

In the last chapter, I mentioned Jacques Delors' four pillars of structure and explored the concept of learning to be and how related it is or was to my early years. Now, I'd like to consider the second of those pillars.

Learning to know is a reflective competence and one that I had not developed enough to be able to comprehend what was going on. My consciousness had been exposed to new information, which had landed in my head like an unexploded bomb, where it had blown into a thousand thoughts and feelings or shrapnel of the mind—conclusions, assumptions, threats, and fears—and although some of what was swirling around in my psyche was not real, the sensations it produced, the experience, was not imagined. I was living in a personal hell, spinning uncontrollably, just like the scene where Dorothy is dropped into a strange world of colour in the classic film *The Wizard of Oz*, except I was not going to land anywhere as magical as Oz.

How was I to make any coherent sense of this, and how could I trust the plausibility of anything that my mother would say to me? This was not a new question. I fully acknowledge that she had lost a husband and deserved to be happy but at what cost and at whose expense? I also questioned the men whom she introduced into the home. My attitude towards them could have been different, but that change had to be driven by them as reflected in their investment in me and my siblings. After all, I was just a wee boy, and from where I was standing, they were only interested in making themselves happy through their relationship with our mother.

The process I went through, albeit unconsciously, can be summed up with this set of principles:

CHANGING THE ROOT

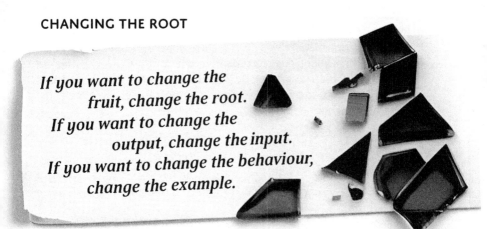

*If you want to change the fruit, change the root.
If you want to change the output, change the input.
If you want to change the behaviour, change the example.*

When I think about that time in my life, I can see that I was responding to the dominance of silence, ignorance or even mistrust, and I recognise that I was transitioning from childlike dependence to knowledge-based adulthood way before my time. I had developed a dominant self-derived mindset and pattern of deep thinking, which had grown from the truth of my direct experiences rather than being based on anything laid down for me.

This culture suited my naturally introverted self, but on reflection, it was not helping me climb out of the emotional ring of steel that I was building around myself. Indeed, it would be some time before I started to deconstruct that structure, a process that, thankfully, I began before it was too late. That said, it never is too late.

CHANGING THE INPUT

I'd decided that if I were to live and prosper in a world where truths and knowledge seemed to be in flux depending on who the source was, I would have to take information from those others with a pinch of salt and assume nothing until clear and unquestionable evidence was provided. Although I did not know this at the time, this was my first baby step to becoming more emotionally intelligent; this was not something on the school curriculum but a powerful lesson, all the same, brought to me by the university (or high school even) of life.

As I grew more independent, I was able to live with the paradox that was the life I had experienced and the life that I discovered. One didn't have to cancel the other, and I learnt how to accept them both as two sides of the same truth. American novelist, essayist and short story writer, Scott Fitzgerald, wrote that 'The test of a first-rate intelligence is the ability to hold two opposed ideas in the mind at the same time and still retain the ability to function.' Well, I was functioning, and I was able to consider and disregard the input from my mother, exorcising the emotional pillaging that had taken my father from me not once but twice.

It was the world that changed, not Dad. Before ground zero, the moment when Mum confirmed that Dad wasn't my biological father, I accepted that he was. That was my reality then. In deciding to embrace the new reality, that he was not my biological father, I was choosing to bury him for the second and final time, and the paradox—that he could be my biological father and not so at the same time—was resolved.

This eureka moment allowed me to move forward with confidence, even if not happily. In drawing a line in the sand, I was choosing to march forward, free from influences that I did not want or recognise as being aligned with my new outlook. I recognised this for what it was—freedom! To be clear, the situation was far from ideal, but the effect was to make me stronger and undoubtedly more resilient, something I was to rely on a lot when I served in the British Army and in my business life.

One of my early challenges was to recognise and accept help when it presented itself. Let me narrate a story I heard once; it has stuck with me for a long time, and I often tell it in learning programmes that I run.

THREE BOATS

A man, who we'll call Graham, was on a river trip in a fast-moving boat when he slipped and fell overboard. Nobody noticed, so he was alone in the water, but since he was a man of faith and believed that God would always look after him, he had become accustomed to never asking for help, relying on himself to get through life.

As he was bobbing in the river, Graham had a thought:

This is not ideal, but I will be okay.
It's an unfortunate situation,
but God will save me.

Just as he was starting to get a bit cold, a boat passed by and stopped near him.

'Let me help you,' said the person rowing the boat. 'Climb aboard.'

But Graham was not interested. 'No, thanks. It's okay. God will save me,' he explained, so the would-be rescuer shrugged his shoulders, bid him farewell, and rowed away.

A little while later, another boat stopped and the skipper offered to help, but Graham once again refused, proclaiming that God would save him. The same thing happened again, and he remained adamant that he would be rescued by God.

Sadly, there could be only one outcome. Graham slipped into hypothermia, lost consciousness, and drowned. When he opened his eyes again, he was hovering outside the Pearly Gates. Saint Peter approached to open the gates to heaven. 'Hold on a minute,' Graham protested. 'I'm not supposed to be here. I want to speak to God before I go anywhere.'

'Certainly,' replied Saint Peter. 'I'll be a couple of ticks,' and off he floated, joyously, not disturbed in the least by the demands of Graham.

When Saint Peter returned, he had God by his side, but before God could say a thing, Graham launched into a bit of an angry rant. 'God, why didn't you save me? I have been faithful to you all my life, and I was waiting for you to save me.'

God remained silent for a few moments.

'Are you finished? Do you want me to send you to Hell? I can sort it now if you want.'

'Um, no. Ahem. Sorry. I have a family down there. May I ask why you didn't save me?'

God smiled reassuringly and lovingly.

'I'm just messing with you, Graham. I knew you were waiting. That's why I sent you three boats.'

Don't do a Graham! Look out for the boats. Sometimes, we are stuck in the complexity and can't see the simplicity!

Nobody knows whether Graham decided to go back to the life he'd known on Earth or chose Heaven.

SELF-BELIEF

This story captures the essence of a mindset that is closed to the capacious nature of knowledge, instead of investing faith in harmony and the paradox of uncertainty: only placing trust in one piece of information, one perspective or one person over another. That was me, except that at the early stages of my life, I had faith and strength but was not clear where to invest it, so I ploughed it all into myself. That's what we do as humans; we turn to the self, especially those of us who have suffered trauma, recognised or not, or, indeed, happen to be strongly introverted.

It can be difficult to navigate as a solo explorer, but when you get to a landmark or a milestone that you recognise, you gain confidence and that is what I was doing. I loved sport, played everything I could get to, loved football and rugby, and found that I fitted into the teams I joined and became a big part of that scene. I did this alone. Nobody came to watch me, and nobody encouraged me, but I did not need anybody to—I was a self-driven boy—but that's not to say it wouldn't have been nice to have someone there. Perhaps, I only got part way to my full potential, I am not sure, but I do wonder, and that is not what I want for anyone. I want everyone to reach their potential, no matter what that looks like. I would far rather have someone on my team who leaves nothing behind than someone who has lots of capability but only gives a fraction.

Sport turned out to be a saviour for me and not because I excelled in my pursuits but because it helped bring out the best in me. It connected me to people who cared for us, coached us, and wanted us to reach our full potential. This also manifested in some of the other elements of my life, particularly school.

JUNIOR HIGH

In Northern Ireland and in the area where I lived, we went to junior high after primary school, for years eight to ten (11–14 years old), and this is when I started to flourish, making great friends, taking part in loads of sporting activities, and thriving socially. Clounagh Junior High School was a happy place, and I settled in very easily and quickly. That school will always hold a special place in my heart, and I have many fond memories of the teachers who taught me, the opportunities I was presented with, and the experiences I had there.

The more perceptive teachers who cared for us could see that although I was a seemingly happy child, there were issues at play. I must admit that I was disruptive at times and a bit of a handful, and this was almost certainly due to frustration more than anything else, as I was highly capable academically but lazy. You could say I lacked motivation, but that's the job of parents, not teachers! Rubbish in, rubbish out!

Maybe if this memoir reaches enough people back home in Portadown, Clounagh Junior High will have me back, and I can tell all those younger versions of me what is out there for them if they lift their heads and open their eyes fully!

Although I flunked out of school at sixteen, I had other things on my mind, and school did not fit with the plan. I later went on to educate myself to master's degree level, but Clounagh Junior High remains home to my favourite memories of any learning institution I have ever had the pleasure of attending.

There is so much more to gain in these formative years of education than learning. In fact, I would argue that learning is the least important benefit of education, but not having the keen interest and investment from one's parents or at least one parent will most probably mean that a child will not reach their full potential and many opportunities will pass them by; sometimes, those opportunities are gone forever.

I was lucky. I managed to achieve despite my earlier lack of motivation. Let's not allow our young people to miss out. Invest, invest, and invest for not only the sake of the children but for society, and don't be the one who tells or, even worse, moans at the youth, 'It was far better in my day,' when the reality is that it probably wasn't!

RECOGNISING THE EXAMPLE

My first boat was sent to me when I was fourteen when I got a job in a local fish-and-chip shop. Keith didn't exactly welcome me, but he gave me a shot, and in life, when you get a shot, especially if you know what you can do with the shot, bust a gut. I did, and Keith very quickly warmed to me and what I could bring to the party or, at least, the chippy.

For the first time in my life, I recognised myself as an adult outside of school and at home. Keith became my mentor and I probably, deep down, wanted him as my father. That, of course, was not going to happen, but I could live the relationship as though he was, and I did! I did everything to please Keith and to build my offering, and I built and built, and Keith played a massive part in that.

The example that Keith set for me was to become reflected in everything that I did—my work ethic, my insistence on standards, and my approach to instilling capability in others by investing in trust and delegation to the lowest level. I later came to know this approach as mission command, a British Army philosophy that is in use all the time, not just in war. Its guiding principle requires the chain of command (boss or line manager) to operate to achieve the higher commander's intent. It promotes decentralisation of decision-making, freedom of action, and initiative. Keith trusted me in the shop alone, at fifteen, and left me his chequebook to pay suppliers!

I am a lifelong subscriber to the idea that the mess we accept becomes our message. It is up to us to fix it or address the root cause and control our mindset; otherwise, we just end up plastering over the problem. My problem was that the mess that I was dealing with was the poor example at home, so it was in my blind spot because I was only aware of the consequences, not the root cause. The moment I walked into the shop and met Keith, I could see the fix and an example of the mindset to which I was naturally drawn. I am going to revisit the theme of natural attraction later.

You can put someone into a new situation, but no good will come out of it if their mindset is closed because it is too set in its ways. Nothing will change until the mindset is treated. What I had was an open, growth mindset, and I was fortunate enough to find a new environment that matched it.

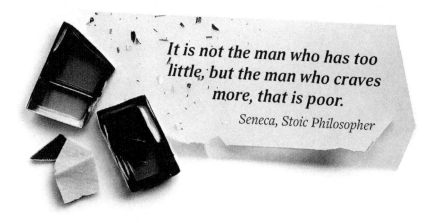

It is not the man who has too little, but the man who craves more, that is poor.

Seneca, Stoic Philosopher

The concept of hedonic adaptation is something that I have come to recognise in my journey, in that I took all the things in my life that were good for granted, not the shiny or emotional stuff but the fact that I was safe, had food, shelter and love. My mother loved us very much, and that was never an issue. I was just a wee boy with a strong undercurrent of ambition and expectation who needed somewhere to invest the energy and perhaps some patience and a little humility for those around him who did not share his outlook.

At that point, I was very happy and planning the next stage of my adventure, independently, yes, but happily, and I could consign the idea of not having a father to the history books, which is where it belonged. It still made an appearance now and again, just like any other historical text, but when it did, I recognised it for what it was.

With that in mind. This is for Robert McNally, my dad.

RIP Dad
Remembered in Providence.
You may not have been there,
but your absence made me what I am.

GOODBYE, IRELAND

From the age of fourteen, I had set my sights on my ticket to real freedom, adventure, and a one-way ticket out of Northern Ireland. Having waited patiently and put the work in to ensure I was ready, my time had come, and I was off to join the British Army. the final chapter of a four-year plan.

It felt like I was riding a wave that I was only slightly aware of, a force at play that I was willing to go with while the direction of travel felt right. It was time to embrace the prize I had worked for.

38

Natural Selection

As dawn broke, I looked across to the hills on my left and was struggling to make out what I was seeing. Was I tired? A week had passed since I had slept for anything more than a few hours at a time. *What is that on the high ground?*

Only a few hours earlier, in the pitch black, the thunder of artillery guns firing overhead had drowned out the night. We were in the final stages of a live-fire training exercise on Salisbury Plain, and as the sun crept higher, throwing more light across the countryside, those blobs on the horizon became easier to identify.

Holy shit! I knew exactly what I was looking at. Sheep! There were about 40 of them scattered across an area around half the size of a football pitch, and they were in pretty poor shape—many were in no shape at all, and others in very strange shapes indeed. As I realised what had happened, I called over the radio and gave the order for everyone to convene on my position once the attack was complete. I got my soldiers to form an all-round defence of the position (360-degree coverage), while the other platoons cleared their positions. Once everyone had gathered round, I took the debrief on the attack.

A GLIMPSE OF THE HORRORS OF WAR

Everyone looked gutted. We were surrounded by blood-soaked dead and dying sheep splayed out on the ground. A farmer had left them out by accident, a mistake that would cost him dearly but had cost the sheep more.

The sound of the artillery guns firing at the start of the attack was deafening—exciting, and even scary—but we were out of harm's way, unlike the sheep, who had congregated right in the epicentre of the impact zone. We were looking at the realities of armed conflict.

Until you've been to war, you don't get to experience the carnage caused by conventional weaponry, but we were given a taste that day. Some of the sheep had been blown to pieces. Others had lost limbs, severed at the joint by gunfire or torn off by the blasts from explosions. Most of them were riddled with bullets. Some were still alive. Hot shrapnel had ploughed through their bodies like hot bearings through butter, leaving gaping wounds you could fit your hand in.

Then there was the stench—the smell of burning flesh, blood, and death. Their sacrifice provided a very clear and valuable lesson about digging in for cover from artillery fire. More than that, we were given a glimpse of what life could be like on a real battlefield except that in this instance, no human blood had been spilt.

It wasn't over. We had a duty to put survivors out of their misery, and the only thing available to us were 5.56 mm bullets, so the injured were euthanised with close-range shots to the head for a quick death.

Who would choose this?

THE PREDICTION MACHINE

It's all about natural attraction. From the age of fourteen, I knew I was heading for the Army and by then, I had built a kind of prediction machine. When I was focused on making something happen, I would instinctively and intuitively sense what to do to achieve it. Anything other than willpower and hard work, I'd source from the outside. The Army suited me, my way of going about things, my attitude, and my attraction towards stability and strong males. The Army was supposed to be the filler for the cracks that had widened with the continued absence of a father in my life; it couldn't do that, but it did something far more meaningful and transformational.

We all have a need and a right to feel fulfilled, don't we? Fulfilled in our social lives, our work lives, and our personal lives. That's what I believe, even if some would say I am being too idealistic. When I decided to chase a career in the Army, I didn't feel fulfilled. Before I met Keith, I didn't have a job either, other than being a student, and although that helped me to grow, it wasn't fulfilling me.

My social situation was no better, although I was fortunate enough not to have fallen foul of the deceit of the social environment of Northern Ireland; by that, I'm talking about The Troubles in which I had grown up—I had never known peace in its truest form. What we called peace in Northern Ireland in the seventies was a far cry from what people in the Republic of Ireland, Scotland, Wales or England would call peace.

AN UNWANTED BIRTHRIGHT

I did not buy into the bias that I was supposed to accept and adopt unconditionally just because of the family I was born into or the programming that weighed on people in my community to be on one side or the other. There was a list of questions that we could expect to be asked at any time, and even if we weren't asked, others were asking it silently without saying so. See if you recognise any of these:

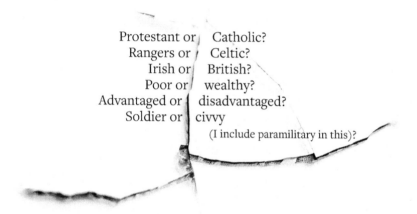

Protestant or Catholic?
Rangers or Celtic?
Irish or British?
Poor or wealthy?
Advantaged or disadvantaged?
Soldier or civvy
(I include paramilitary in this)?

Interestingly, there were very few Black or other non-white people in Northern Ireland at the time, and who would want to come to the region? We did have a small community of Black, Chinese, and Indian families, and I was very lucky to have a good friend from each of these communities, but it was not easy for them; they faced the same questions as the rest of us and then had all the race-related questions to contend with on top.

Like race or nationality, for most of us in Northern Ireland, religion wasn't something we got to choose and once that was determined, our preferred football club followed by default. This prison we were born into was an unwanted birthright. The only way that I was going to be able to break completely free from the shackles of these non-choices was to leave.

The constraints that went with living in Northern Ireland during The Troubles were not my only reason for wanting to join the Army.

41

I could see adventure, freedom, and opportunity; and even at that early age, I knew my personality would be a perfect match.

GATHERING TOOLS

While biding my time until I was old enough to enlist, I got my head down, worked hard, built up my skillset, and prepared myself mentally for my departure from my home, and day by day, I was strengthening my prediction machine to guarantee success in the Army. During that time, three of my closest friends joined up ahead of me, and the toughest one of them was home in six weeks. They couldn't cut it. That would never be me, and I was sure of that.

Being raised in Northern Ireland was excellent preparation for facing basic training in arguably the best military in the world. If I could survive the streets of Portadown, avoid getting trapped in the wrong place, and keep a smile on my face, I was likely to be okay in the British Army!

CHARACTER MEANS GIVING IT YOUR ALL

I left school at sixteen with a few paltry GCSEs, which was something I came to regret later when it sunk in that I had failed to achieve my potential. These days, I believe that failing to achieve one's potential is what Christians call a sin, a transgression against divine law, and I have far more respect for someone who gives it everything but achieves less than someone who doesn't put everything in but achieves more. Putting in maximum effort shows character. The one who fails to give it everything will always fail to fulfil their potential.

I never failed to give it everything I had in Keith's chippy and worked every shift available until the last week before joining the Army. That reminds me of another example of my prediction machine, my final words to Keith: 'Thanks for everything. When I come back to Northern Ireland, it will be to buy this place.'

I was eighteen with a grand in the bank, and Keith's was the busiest fast-food shop in the town, worth an estimated quarter of a million pounds even then or over half a million pounds in today's terms. *Did I do that?!* The earliest predictor is a person's mindset. Get that right and your mindset will become a prediction machine.

FROM CIVVY TO SOLDIER

It was a typically chilly morning on Monday, 4 March 1991. The number-one record in the UK's music charts was The Clash's 'Should I Stay, or Should I Go?' and it was all I ever heard whenever

I was within earshot of a radio. That was an easy choice for me. I was going or rather, I'd already gone.

As the train pulled into Darlington station, I stood in the aisle with a heart full of hope, anticipation, and nervous excitement. The hustle and bustle, the distinctive smell that you only get in train stations, and a rucksack full of all the gear I'd been told to bring—the Army gives very specific instructions on what items to pack—just added to the sense that my prediction machine had worked, and I was going places.

For the previous few hours, I'd shared a carriage with other fresh recruits, and not a word had been spoken by anyone. I'm not a mind reader, so I can only guess what was going on in other people's heads. Some would have been crapping themselves, for sure, overwhelmed with the sense that they had reached the point of no return, like that part of a roller coaster ride moments before the big drop, and others would have thought about the lives they were leaving behind. Then, there was me, and my focus was on where we were going and what was going to happen next. I felt as nervous as the rest of them, but I am not sure whether it was fear—I was ready for anything. I had chosen this.

SHOUTING, QUEUES, AND MORE QUEUES

As soon as I stepped off the train, I spotted the uniformed corporal waiting for us, and I couldn't wait to shake his hand. I offered him mine and although he accepted, there was a non-plussed expression on his face. We weren't entering into a business contract. His job was to knock me and the other recruits into shape, and it was not intended to be a pleasant experience.

The next few hours were a blur of lots of shouting, bustling, bags getting dropped, and getting into lines; queueing in lines turned out to be a regular occurrence from this point. I was placed into my troop, which is a formation of soldiers comprising three sections of around ten troops each, so I knew who I was going to be bleeding, sweating, and weeping with over the next ten weeks.

We were introduced to the three corporals who would be responsible for guiding us through our basic training—an interesting experience indeed. The Army has its own version of good-cop bad-cop, with a friendly supportive trainer, a harsher one that everyone immediately knows not to cross, and another who floats between the two extremes. At the time, we didn't know what was going on. We were just kids really, and if they said jump, we'd aim as high as we could. Reflecting on it now, I can see it for what it was—a slick operation, carefully designed and choreographed to get the most out of every soldier.

When you think about what the Army needs to achieve—to prepare rough and ready youngsters from a range of backgrounds for working together as an efficient machine, ready to pull a trigger and kill on command if necessary—it's much easier to make sense of its approach to basic training. Whatever beliefs and attitudes recruits have held while in civvy street must be carefully stripped away without taking away their essence and potential as soldiers, so they can be rebuilt as the perfect team players, ready for whatever situation the Army needs them for. It takes a meticulously planned campaign to pull that off, and our three corporals were past masters. The Army identifies the strengths, weaknesses and potential of every recruit and fine-tunes them for optimum performance as soldiers.

GRAB YOUR KIT

Our first task was to collect our military uniform or kit as it is more commonly referred to. If you have served, you will recognise this unique and unforgettable experience. The ambience of an Army clothing store is unlike anything I ever encountered since or before—the smell and a feeling that is wet and dry, warm and cold, reassuring and scary all at once.

They literally threw gear at us as we were ushered through the process like cars on a conveyor belt. Catch. Move on. Next. We weren't shopping for suits in Savile Row after all. Everything about military life is quick and efficient. There's no time to waste, and there's always something to do.

They issued us with boots that I am convinced were the inspiration for the saying tough as old boots. I guess anything we were going to be wearing for sixteen hours a day, especially doing the stuff we were going to do, would have to be built to last. They weren't built for comfort; that's for sure.

On return to our lines (the accommodation that would become home), we had to change immediately into our new kit and put our civvies away in a room, not to be seen again until the end of week six, unless anyone 'biffed it' (the military term for leaving the Army without completing the training).

BUILDING SOLDIERS

For some, British Army basic training is the toughest challenge they would have faced in their lives. It turned out to be run-of-the-mill for me. It was hard, and the conditions were extreme, but I had prepared mentally and physically. More than that, I was supposed to be here, so my attitude and mindset accepted everything that was thrown at us as part of a plan, just another step. Acceptance is one of the keys to overcoming adversity. Owning it empowers you. It is much more difficult to process something uncomfortable that you haven't asked for or accepted.

For others, it was too much, and they fell by the wayside. One of those who struggled was Jones. He could not stand straight, could not iron his kit, and was constantly in a shit state, an Army phrase that was regularly belted out by officers when Jones was around. His lack of discipline and attention to detail meant he was constantly having to stand for show parade, the Army's punishment for not being dressed well enough for the regular parade.

These soldiers would be made to parade at the guard room at 2200 hours to be inspected, an exercise designed to put them under further pressure. Jones was not a natural but that said, he was a good lad, which the corporals recognised, so they tolerated him a bit more than others, but he needed to shape up if he was going to meet the required standards. What did they do to help him get there? They made him my responsibility!

Jones was put in my room and the corporals told me that I would do his show parades if he was not up to standard, which effectively meant that I had to do my kit and his. It may seem harsh to civilians, but it is a simple concept really; the lesson being that if we look after each other in peace, we will look after each other in battle.

The other subliminal lesson that ran through everything we did was the importance of trust-building, not the kind of trust we see in civilian life of being able to count on someone else to do a simple job but the absolute, unconditional trust in the commands we were issued and in those who issued them. On the flip side, our commanding officers expected that we would execute those tasks without compromise.

We were given very strict instructions when in barracks, so everyone knew what was expected of them and there was no room for misunderstanding. The last thing you want in battle is ambiguity, so one thing you notice in the military is the clarity of every communication. One of the guidelines we were given was to have lights out by 2200 hours. You can see why having to attend show parade was so much of a pain in the arse. It was almost impossible to finish kit prep by that time, so most of us would either be under our beds ironing clothes by torchlight or polishing our boots on the mat at the side of our bed or reading for the next day.

Although this was not allowed, it was tolerated to a degree to allow us to recognise the importance of getting our shit done on time. Given that our days started at 0600 hours, it wasn't in anyone's best interests to stay up a minute longer than necessary.

What was not tolerated was the use of washing machines or dryers after lights out. Getting your kit washed was always a massive burden and often, you might have got it washed but not dried and would have to wear it wet—clean but wet. The washer and dryer were in a room directly opposite mine, but even their proximity did not tempt me to use them for fear of the consequences. In the Army, when one person drops the ball, everyone gets punished, and I didn't want to risk that being inflicted on my fellow soldiers. That didn't matter to Signaller Kilkenny though, one of the soldiers in my dorm, and he thought it was okay to put his kit in the washer after the 2200 hours deadline one night.

I heard the racket and poked my head out of my room: 'Fuck's sake, mate. What are you playing at?' He was determined to do whatever he could to avoid show parade and thought he would get away with it. There wasn't much I could do and besides, he was a good guy, a funny bloke, so although I was pissed off that he was taking a risk on behalf of all of us, I wound my head back into my room, went back to bed, and hoped for the best.

Sure enough, the duty corporal, who must have had extra-sensory perception, heard the washing machine and came into the lines. Whenever they entered the lines, they would shout 'Corridor!' This was our prompt to come out and line up along the walls. He grabbed Kilkenny and quizzed him about the rule governing the use of the cleaning machines. Kilkenny had no choice but to admit that he knew them, and that would mean having to take responsibility for breaking them.

'Kilkenny,' he said, 'it's okay. I understand how it is. We've all been there. You have to get your kit ready for parade, and there ain't enough hours in the day. I get it. I really do.'

What the fuck just happened? You could almost hear the jaw of every soldier in the corridor dropping to the floor. I mean this corporal was, to put it bluntly, a proper nasty bastard. At least, that was the role he played. He was the Mr Nasty of the trio. Was he going to let Kilkenny off the hook?

'Signaller Kilkenny, I understand the pressure you are under, so I am going to let you wash your kit on this occasion, but here's how it is going to work.'

Kilkenny was standing as upright as he could, eyes popping

out of his head and managing to maintain his composure, but he was starting to realise that Corporal Nasty was about to deliver a punchline.

'You will stand on top of the machine between now and reveille at 0600 hours. McNally, every time that cycle stops, you put it back on.' Reveille is the name for the sound of the bugle to indicate it's time to get up for parade, so neither Kilkenny nor I were going to get any sleep that night. *Cheers, mate!*

By the time the bugle sounded, Kilkenny was in clip order (Army slang for being tired and disorientated), having stood for eight hours on top of the washing machine; at least he had a clean but wet kit. I can assure you that no one ever put the washing machine on after the deadline again—tough, but lesson learnt!

NATURAL ATTRACTION

I first became aware of the concept of natural attraction as an officer cadet later in my career when I read Lord Moran's very powerful account of the psychological effects of war on soldiers, *The Anatomy of Courage*, which drew primarily from his experience and observations from World War One. It was one of several books that I was required to read while studying and training at Sandhurst.

Despite the challenges of basic training, I thrived because I was always able to frame whatever stood in my way as a stepping stone, and again, most importantly, it was my choice, and I loved it. What I was witnessing all around me, which *The Anatomy of Courage* later confirmed, was the process of weeding out those who do not have the character or temperament to fight when the time comes. How do you do that? How does the Army do that?

The Army's approach is simple. You work them hard, physically and mentally, endeavour to expose weaknesses that either break or build the will of the recruit, introduce danger, and test their character repeatedly. This process of testing and building up increases the resilience of recruits and produces well-trained, disciplined, and reliable soldiers. I was naturally attracted to the Army because I was naturally made for it.

DISCIPLINE

There will be many scholarly articles that explain discipline much more eloquently than I ever could, but for me, in those early years, it was very simple—discipline was a mindset. The Army was the best place for me, and I wanted to do my best; that meant following the instructions I was given and trusting that they were right and fit for the purpose they were designed for.

Discipline is probably the stand-out characteristic that people most strongly associate with military service, particularly the British military, given its history and record. Fundamentally, discipline is easy if you have a passion for what you are doing. The work we do should drive our passion and be driven by our passion and for anyone whose work does not talk to their passion, I can say without any doubt that they will be able to recount times when they have not been disciplined in delivering whatever was expected. When you question your Why, you challenge your discipline.

For me, discipline is about accepting responsibility for yourself and for those whom you either lead professionally or command militarily. You are responsible for everything that occurs in your organisation from the lowest level even when delegating responsibility. Our behaviours and consistency are what set the disciplined apart from the ill-disciplined.

A friend of mine once told me that 'Discipline is doing the right thing even when you know nobody is looking.' And this is right, as discipline is not something to turn on for an audience. It is an intrinsic character trait that sets us apart. It can be learnt, but the conditions must be conducive. It took discipline for me to craft a path out of Northern Ireland, and I took steps over a prolonged period. Militarily, it is about drilling behaviours and instincts, so they become second nature. For many others, it is about sticking to the task personally and professionally. No matter what your approach or attitude towards discipline is, it will help you through the challenges that cause many to fail.

MY WHY

Although I was naturally attracted to the Army and, once I had joined, very quickly learnt what the Army was all about and how to be successful within its ranks, it was the deep connection with my Why that allowed me to thrive in this tough environment. When I reflect on why I so desperately wanted to join the Army and why the extreme regime did not bother me, I can see that my Why was freedom, and leaving Northern Ireland was the way to gain it—freedom from the divides that existed in my community, freedom from the memories of losing my father at such a young age and never really being able to fill the gap, and the freedom to explore the world. That Why was enough to get me through anything.

One night, on exercise, during the first ten weeks of training, I was lying in a shell scrape, which is a hole you dig in the ground when you know you're going to be static for a while. Shell scrapes only need to be around eighteen inches deep as their purpose is to provide enough protection to shield you from shrapnel.

It was a chilly night, and I was freezing my bollocks off. As I looked out towards a far-off road and saw the headlights of a car, I imagined how great it would be to be sat inside it with the heating on. But before that thought could take hold in my mind, another one took command of the situation:

No! Being in that car would mean you are not here, and being here is part of your journey. This is your escape from Northern Ireland and your ticket to freedom.

It was my Why reminding me why it was a sensible idea to lie down in the cold instead of snuggling up in bed with someone warm and beautiful. I was freezing because I had not unpacked my sleeping bag or warm kit as I knew we would not get to settle in and would have to bug out—Army-speak for move to a new location. They did this to keep us awake and see how we performed under extreme tiredness. I wanted to be alert and ready to move, so I did everything to make sure that I could move at the drop of a hat.

Sure enough, we were bugged out, and I made it to the next checkpoint ahead of everyone. Corporal Nasty was waiting at the checkpoint, and he looked a bit bewildered. 'Fuck me, McNally. How did you get here so quickly?'

'My kit was already packed, and I was ready to move instantly, corporal.' I could see his mind working.

'Were you in your sleeping bag?'

There was no point lying about it.

'No. It was packed, corporal.'

What he said next has stuck with me for thirty years, and I have said it many times myself (minus the expletive): 'McNally, any c**t can be uncomfortable.' With that, he walked on.

Why did I lie there in the cold? Well, I thought that if I failed any part of basic training, I would be sent back to Northern Ireland, and there was no way I was going to let that happen. My Why blotted out the cold, magnified my resolve, and kept me laser-focused. My Why was bigger than me and bigger than the challenges that lay before me. What I was doing and how I was doing it was no more than a means to an end. That was simply the mechanical manifestation of my vision of the life I was creating for myself.

DO YOU KNOW YOUR WHY?

Life is tough and becoming more complex as we enter a world of ever-increasing economic polarisation and the inequalities that this causes. This has been exacerbated by the COVID-19 pandemic; the world of work and life has shifted at a pace never seen before, and we must navigate this on many levels—at work, in the family, and within our social tribes. If we are not guided by our Why, we will struggle for meaning and purpose.

Although it has morphed over the years, I was guided by my Why from a young age, and I have been driven by a purpose ever since. Every action taken was focused on that purpose, every outcome was aimed at the purpose, and the results were measured against my purpose-driven life. That's not to say there haven't been some wobbles along the way.

I continued to flourish in the Army. Basic training was tough, but I didn't find it difficult. Indeed, I was able to help others who were struggling. We sometimes laughed a lot at the adversity and other times at what we saw unfolding around us. I remember one incident very fondly, and it brings a smile to my face if not a giggle when I relive it.

FIND TIME TO LAUGH

It was a sunny afternoon, and we were sitting in a warm classroom. Although study days were a little more laid back than working in the field or being drilled in the square, it was easy to get struck by that nodding dog feeling, when your head keeps dropping as you fight the urge to sleep. Going to sleep in a military classroom is not something I would recommend. One of our troops, Burke, was permanently battered, and his head would start nodding every time we were in the classroom.

The corporal spotted Burke's head nodding and warned him to stay awake, but poor Burke, bless him, kept drifting and could not snap out of it, so the corporal had to give him a second warning. His head dropped again but this time, it didn't bounce back up. Burke was out for the count. I was sitting quite close to him, doing my best not to burst out laughing, but I could see the corporal was getting a bit agitated. Then, it happened.

In the blink of an eye, the corporal launched the wooden blackboard duster at Burke's head with surgical precision. The projectile flew towards Burke like a laser-guided missile and connected perfectly with the centre of his forehead. If you can't remember or don't know what the old chalk dusters looked like, let me assure you that they were quite dense, chunky objects, and the dull thud that echoed from Burke's head is as fresh in my mind today as it was in

1991 when Vic Reeves and The Wonder Stuff released their aptly named number-one track, 'Dizzy'.

The impact of that duster definitely left Burke's head spinning, and he had no clue what had hit him as he bolted upright, rudely awakened from his temporary slumber. God knows what he had been dreaming about, but waking up to a barrage from the corporal must have felt like the stuff of nightmares for the poor guy. I couldn't hold it any longer and burst out laughing. That triggered the whole classroom to erupt, and it even mellowed the corporal who gave way to a small smile, which was probably the best outcome for Burke.

Even when things are tough, look for the laughs, hang on to the Why, and keep moving forward. I was living my best life, learning, meeting new mates, and facing challenges that opened my eyes to what I was capable of. I went on to serve for another sixteen years, and I will be sharing and exploring more of my military experiences in the coming chapters.

THE WHY CAN CHANGE

Since leaving regular service, I have served as a reserve officer, amassing over twenty years of military experience to date. After working so hard to free myself of the chains of Northern Ireland, I've gone full circle and now live there.

Northern Ireland is a beautiful place, full of beautiful people. It was the situation I faced in Northern Ireland in the seventies and eighties that I wanted to leave, and a lot has changed since then. It's a different place now—not perfect but different.

In life, if you are fortunate enough to recognise your Why and your purpose, go with it, trust your instinct, and it will reward you. Build stories through experiences, be open to new things and new people, and be the person you needed to have around you when the going was tough.

Remember that your Why can change as your circumstances change, or you may have to find a new Why if you manage to achieve your goals. What counts is that you know what your Why is today and allow natural attraction to take you where you need to be.

In the next chapter, I'm going to be looking at how to lead others to help them reach their potential.

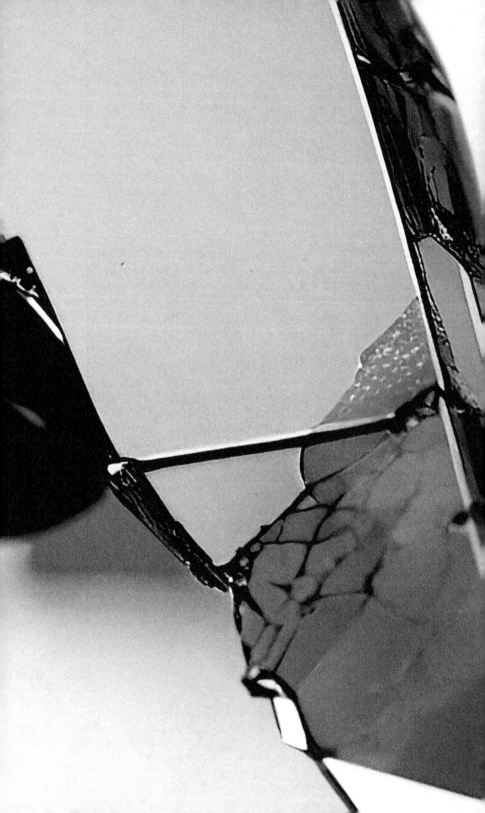

Avoiding Unintended Consequences

Communication is one of the most essential skills for leadership. When we give written or verbal instructions to others, how can we ensure that the message we want to convey is the one that is received? Even if it is, is it the right message to achieve the objective?

This chapter looks at communication through the lens of leadership, expectations, and outputs. Let's explore what it means to set expectations and how doing so affects how teams and individuals perform.

LEARNING FROM PROBLEMS

I have spent a lot of time being trained and delivering training to others throughout my military career and more recently in my current role as a learning lead for one of the Big Four UK-based business consultancies, although I have never really classed myself as a learning expert—more a performance consultant interested in helping my stakeholders find solutions to complex problems.

It's a simple concept, but the answers people are looking for are often more likely to come when they are presented with further problems rather than solutions. We will go into more detail on problem-solving later. For now, let's accept that, typically, people fall in love with their solution; it's a love affair that, like many marriages, falls apart at the first sign of a test. That's why I prefer to deliver memorable challenges that people will connect with emotionally and learn from. This isn't something that I was taught, but it was an approach that felt intuitively right and proved to be increasingly fruitful with experience.

Whenever I was charged with delivering training or facilitating a workshop, much to the frustration of those around me (and sometimes to me), I'd start by breaking the course and seeing what it looked like when I built it back up. Was the new version transformational? If not, how could we make it so?

CLEAR, REALISTIC EXPECTATIONS

As an Army officer, I have always had a responsibility to design and deliver training for the troops under my command. In a discussion about setting expectations, I can think of many stand-out moments, but the one that comes to mind most frequently highlights the importance of being clear about expectations and especially being realistic.

During my second tour of duty in Northern Ireland as a young officer, I was the second-in-command (2IC or 2i/c) of a company (an infantry company is a collective of about one hundred soldiers). As captain, which is second to major (the company commander), I was responsible for all aspects of training for my troops. I always wanted to deliver training that not only challenged but engaged the men and would often seek their input into what we were going to do and how we would do it. This way, they felt that they were part of the process and not just having stuff dumped on them. In my corporate world, this is called human-centred design and is quite the thing apparently. Who would have known?

AN EXCITING EXERCISE

We were on the ranges for the weekend, and I wanted to put a bit of spice into our exercises. One of the operations that we used to conduct was to mount searches of urban or rural areas of interest. By areas of interest, I mean those places where our intelligence people would tell us there was a high probability of weapons being hidden—ready for use against us if the opportunity arose. Over the years, although we didn't take all the weapons off the streets, we enjoyed some successes. Those we recovered, if not linked to a terrorist incident and taken for evidence, would be stored in our armouries for either training our search personnel or sniffer dogs.

We were occasionally given clearance to use those weapons on our ranges, so I planned to let the soldiers use some of the sawn-off shotguns on a range lane—a line for the troops to patrol down and fire on enemy targets.

I set up two lanes in parallel, so the soldiers could run down the lanes in pairs. They would be using shotguns for a few of the targets before switching to a pistol for the remainder. *Very nice*, I thought and as the range officer in charge, I was satisfied that this would be an exciting way to get the men fired up.

FUCK'S SAKE, BILLY. KEEP UP!

The men were briefed on how to conduct themselves safely on the range and given detailed instructions on how the exercise was to be carried out. My staff were told which soldiers they would be shadowing, and I chose to run with a soldier called Billy.

We were on opposite sides of a sandy berm, which was covered in high grass, so visibility was not ideal, but we were close enough to use sound signals. Billy was a great soldier but had gained a few pounds and was more Pot Billy than Sport Billy. Still, no one was going to have to run like Linford Christie or Usain Bolt because the focus of the challenge was going to be the shooting. I had high expectations that this range would be a great experience for the men. By the way, I ought to add at this point that you will often hear me refer to the soldiers as my men or my boys, and that's not because of any kind of sexism on my part but a reflection of the fact that there were no females in the infantry.

'Billy,' I said before we kicked off the first pair, 'all you have to do is keep within your arcs of fire and stay parallel with me. OK?'

'No bother, boss,' came the response. I didn't believe in being arsey about being called Sir, and boss was fine.

The signal was given, and off we went. The first pair were moving down the lane at pace. The targets popped up, and there was a massive bang as the first round to be discharged came from the barrel of a shotgun. The mark was blasted with shot. *Brilliant*. It was all going to plan. As we progressed down the lane, my guy switched to the pistols for the last few rounds.

A few seconds later, I shouted 'Stop' to end the lane for both soldiers, and we regrouped at the start line for a debrief. I was pleased to say it had worked really well, and it was clear that they'd enjoyed the lane training. Billy was sweating a bit, but I would have been more shocked if he weren't—the sun was shining, and these guys were running around in heavy-duty boots with Kevlar helmets and full body armour.

'Ready to go again, Billy?' He gave a quick nod of the head, and we were off for round two. The first shot rang out from Billy's shotgun, and the round hit the target. *Wonderful. Great shooting, Billy.* I looked across and could just see Billy's head and shoulders through the long grass as I pushed on to the next target.

What the fuck was that? I was suddenly knocked forward by what felt like a dumbbell smashing into my left shoulder. Recovering my composure, I looked back and sure enough, Billy had fallen behind, which confirmed exactly what I suspected had happened. I slowed down, so he could catch up and let him get a little ahead of me. We finished the drill, and it was back to the start line again.

UNINTENDED CONSEQUENCES

'Billy, can I have a word?' I asked as I stepped away from the group, and he followed me. 'How do you think that went?'

'Good,' he declared proudly, clearly oblivious to how close he had come to blowing my head off.

'Fuck's sake, Billy. I told you to keep up.' I said, trying to keep a lid on my feelings of shock. Sometimes, actions speak louder than words, so I took my combat jacket off and presented it to Billy. The grouping of around twenty small holes on the back of the left shoulder should have told him all he needed to know, but he still needed a nudge: 'Billy, the fucking shotgun round hit me.'

My body armour had done its job, and the long grass had slowed the shot down a little, so it only gave me a bit of a kick and some holes in my jacket, but it could have been a lot worse. Long grass or not, a shot to the head would have been no fun at all. Billy was indeed sorry that it had happened, but it was not his fault, not his alone anyway.

If it was any one person's fault, it was mine for not considering the consequences of Billy not being able to keep up, which should have been easy to foresee given that he was a portly chap. The Army ran a poster campaign around that time with the headline 'Too Fat to Fight'. Not sensitive, I admit, but in Billy's case it was true; he was too fat to fight, and I had not considered this properly before commencing the exercise.

I had allowed my enthusiasm for a great range experience for my soldiers to overshadow any consideration for my safety and the safety of other support staff. That should not have happened, but being shot in the shoulder was the wake-up call I needed to ensure that it would never happen again.

Exercises with live rounds are dangerous. Lots of soldiers have died on training exercises, and although it never happened on my watch, I still had the unpleasant task of having to knock on the door of a soldier's family home and tell a mother that her son had been killed by accident, and it was brutal—a horrendous experience. Let's take a moment to reflect on those who have lost their lives in service of any kind—sons, daughters, brothers, sisters, mothers, and fathers.

56

CAUSE AND EFFECT

When I think about the cause of me being shot (albeit lightly) by one of my soldiers, I can see that I did not communicate my expectations clearly enough. Sure, I told Billy to keep up, but what does that mean? More importantly, what did it mean to Billy? As far as he was concerned, he was being asked to move fast enough to stay in line with me and keep us on schedule, but that was all. He was not asked to consider why that was important, and I didn't tell him.

'Keep up' for Billy could have meant pull your finger out, keep moving, or push harder, whereas for me, it meant something altogether different—if he didn't keep up, there was a chance I could get shot. I understood that. He didn't. That's the message I should have communicated to him. That's the expectation—'If you don't keep up, Billy, you might end up shooting me.'

Being shot by Billy is an example of an extreme outcome or effect, but the principle is the same in any scenario. If expectations are not spelt out clearly and accurately, things can go wrong.

FALLING IN LOVE WITH THE SOLUTION

Let me share another water story with you. A man was walking alongside a fast-flowing river when he heard someone calling out for help. He spotted a man in the water, clearly in distress, and jumped in to rescue him and pull the guy to safety. Happy to see that the guy was a little shaken but all right, he continued with his walk.

After only a couple of hundred metres or so, he heard another call for help. This time, it was a woman who was struggling. He jumped in and pulled her to safety. Again, he made sure she was all right before moving on, but the rescue missions were taking their toll, and he was starting to feel quite tired.

A short distance up the trail, he heard another call for help. *What's wrong with these people? Why dive in the river if you can't swim?* This time, it was two children. By the time he had pulled them to safety, he was exhausted. If he found anyone else in the river, there'd be nothing he could do as he barely had enough energy left to walk, let alone start rescuing people.

As he set off, one of the kids, still recovering from their ordeal, called out to him, but it was too late. He didn't hear them and carried on upstream, eventually finding his way to a bridge. Another man was standing at the bridge, staring at the water rushing underneath him and minding his own business. The man suddenly dived at our hero and threw him off the bridge and into the river where he drowned.

If only he had questioned why so many people were struggling in the water and asked the other four people he had rescued, he would have known about the man on the bridge. Sadly, by the time he learnt the truth, it was too late, he was too tired to swim, and there was no one around to rescue him. He fell in love with the solution, saving people, and failed to address or even identify the real problem—a maniac throwing people into the river.

Most of us have made the mistake of falling in love with a solution that we have come up with for a problem, proud of ourselves for solving the issue and for being able to roll out our solution, only to find out that it doesn't work. It's not surprising when you think about it; we have a problem that we desperately want to solve, so when a light switches on, we often grab the first solution with both hands without testing it or even asking the basic questions. We've answered *a* question but not *the* question. When the man saved those people from the water, he was answering a question—how can I save these people from drowning—but he wasn't answering *the* question: Why are all these people in the water? He had assumed, mistakenly, that they had a choice.

ANSWER THE FUCKING QUESTION

Situations like this are what soldiers call answer the fucking question (ATFQ) moments, the fucking question being the one you really ought to be asking. This question gets you to the root cause rather than just alleviating the symptoms. The way to get to the source is to ask as many questions as possible and assume nothing.

I have learnt to max out my ATFQ moments to test my hypothesis and benefitted greatly by doing so. The irony is that we all get this when we're toddlers. They rarely accept the first answer they're given—'But why, Mummy?'—but then we grow out of it; perhaps we shouldn't.

We'll look at some more examples of ATFQ moments in the next chapter. For now, imagine this: a builder is contracted to build a very specific house for a client, but he isn't given any detailed plans or instructions. This is a recipe for disaster, and, unfortunately, this is also what employees experience when leaders don't provide them with clear team expectations.

According to a study from Gallup[1], only half of the employees surveyed said they knew what their workplace expectations were. Billy knew he needed to keep up with me, but he didn't know why or how he was going to do this. My solution was orientated towards the participants having a great experience on the range, not the supporting staff. I let them down by not digging deeper into why and how for Billy. I failed to ask the important question!

MISSION COMMAND

Setting clear expectations is an essential management skill for building a culture of quality work and accountability.

Uncertainty about roles and expectations leads to poor performance, high stress, and disengagement. That's why it is critical that providing clear expectations for their team, right down to an individual level, when necessary, becomes a reflex for managers. That does not necessarily mean that they have lots of separate conversations with individuals. That could prove to be too time-consuming for a manager, but leaders can employ a concept called mission command.

Mission command is a British Army philosophy that requires everyone to achieve the superior's commander's intent. It is the end objective that needs to be passed down from one level of leadership to the next, so those on the front line understand why they are being asked to do what they are being asked to do. They understand the important question.

This approach promotes the idea of decentralised decision-making and gives others the freedom to act in line with the boss's requirements. Mission command relies on trust and mutual understanding of the tasks to be achieved at all levels and importantly, promotes growth and builds capability across the team and the organisation.

WHAT ARE THE DIFFERENT TYPES OF TEAM EXPECTATIONS, AND WHY ARE THEY IMPORTANT?

Simply put, team expectations are what you anticipate and expect from your team, whether that relates to the quality of work, behaviours, or collaboration appetite.

Expectations bring opportunity, options, and multiple directions of travel, especially when you employ mission command in your leadership offering. They create accountability and can unite a team or company around a shared goal or objective, the Why.

Lack of clarity around expectations can be a fatal flaw in management. If people aren't sure what to work on or what good looks like, you leave success up to chance, risking damaging relationships and eroding confidence and morale. Employees who don't know whether they're on the right path can easily feel unmotivated and disengaged.

There are many categories of expectations, and they are all equally important for high-performing teams but apply to different circumstances or environments.

These categories include:

- Team performance based on business objectives or outcomes
- Individual performance
- Group and individual behaviour based on shared values
- Work quality, processes, and methodology
- Work hours, time off, meetings, and accessibility

If any of these expectations are not clearly understood, you run the risk of uncertainty. Remember, teams expect leaders to deliver clarity regardless of the complexity of the situation. If, for instance, you do not define deadlines and key results, the team is likely to miss deliverables.

Alternatively, if norms around behaviour and values are not defined, solidified, and shared with all team members, it can hinder collaboration and relationships. Consequently, engagement levels and performance are at risk of erosion.

The most dangerous thing you can do as a leader is to assume that what is clear in your head is also clear to your team. I did not tell Billy enough about why I needed him to carry out my instructions. Believe me, getting shot in the shoulder is not a great way to discover why expectations are important!

What do effective team expectations look like?

- Be on time for meetings and briefings.
- Send a detailed agenda for all meeting invites and perhaps make briefing notes available post meeting.
- Be accountable for your mistakes and share your learnings. Do this quickly after the event, so that it does not lose impact.
- Take the initiative to review important information before asking a question, do your homework, and bring the data.
- Break the work down into increments or milestones, and build value at every level.
- Be respectful and clear when giving feedback[2]—feedback is a privilege, and you should aim to do no harm with it; if you do, you will close this very powerful channel down.
- Have a learning mindset—farm for dissent.
- Be present—how many examples have you seen of people listening without hearing or observing without seeing? Be present, be present, and be present!

- Prioritise the team's success before your own—service before self.
- Ask questions when something is not clear for you or you feel it may not be clear for others—as a leader, you carry the responsibility to seek simplicity from complexity.
- Raise flags when you see a blocker, risk, or issue.
- Strive to understand all points of view before challenging them, but remember it is okay to challenge—if it is not, the leadership/management climate is not okay.

HOW TO APPROACH SETTING CLEAR EXPECTATIONS

We know what clear expectations look like and why setting them is important, but is there a process we can use? Every situation is different, but several key considerations will help managers develop the skill of setting clear expectations.

DOCUMENT YOUR TEAM'S PURPOSE AND ROLE

Remember that your team has a brief/mission/statement of works or whatever format your company uses. Treat the team as a single body of the organisation and give them clear direction on what the end state needs to look like (not how to do it but what it needs to look like and achieve). Doing this helps define your team's specific and general outcomes as they relate to greater business objectives.

Write out a clear reporting structure for people, roles, tasks, and core responsibilities—this governance model is critical to the decision-making process. Empower your team within this structure, and give them the freedoms to exercise their skills in getting the job done.

COLLABORATIVELY OUTLINE
TEAM PRINCIPLES AND VALUES

Ask your team to reflect on a set of values to live by. Use these values to solidify behavioural expectations within the team to build cohesion; this is sometimes referred to as contracting. It is important to then commit to putting your expectations into words as a reminder of what has been agreed and to help ensure that the contract is followed.

DEFINE YOUR EXPECTATIONS
AROUND KEY PRIORITIES AND ISSUES

It's one thing to ask your team to deliver a project and another to outline your expectations and quality standards. If you are not clear about this, your team may need to redo the work to fit your vision. Work smart and explain your expectations clearly from the inception:

'Billy, I need you to keep up with me on my lane. Otherwise, there is a risk that your firer will cross my arch and I will be in the firing zone.' This would have been better than allowing Billy to think he needed to keep up so we could finish on time and keep to our schedule.

SET CLEAR MILESTONES FOR GOALS WITH ACTION ITEMS

To help teams work toward big projects, break them down into milestones and action items. A milestone is a mile-marker of progress, such as completing the draft of a training plan. An action item is a specific to-do item, such as getting another team's feedback on the draft design or meeting to discuss the next steps.

COMMUNICATE YOUR EXPECTATIONS
EFFECTIVELY AND INTENTIONALLY

Use storytelling to make an impact. Employees are more likely to remember anecdotes than bullet points. When communicating in person, storytelling helps to contextualise your expectations. You can do this by illustrating what success looks like. Then, reinforce why it matters. A bigger picture helps your team learn about your perspective and expectations. This comes naturally to me now, and I have grown a bank of live examples that I can draw from when appropriate, and the story of Billy is one of them.

ASK YOUR TEAM TO REPEAT WHAT THEY HAVE HEARD

Double-check that everyone has understood what you meant, by asking them to repeat the expectations back to you. You can and should also encourage them to ask questions, or you can ask them questions, and get them to share their understanding of expectations with the group. This allows you to clarify anything that got lost in translation before teams begin the work. You are looking for understanding at a deep level without which you will not be able to let them get on with the work at hand.

REVIEW EXPECTATIONS FREQUENTLY

In general, it's best to test understanding and repeat your expectations often and in different ways, either verbally or with written documentation for example. As things change for your team or within it, you want to reiterate your expectations within the new context. Be sure that all documents are easily accessible and written concisely; jargon doesn't generally work, and the same goes for vernacular language unless everyone understands it—keep it simple, silly (KISS).

CLEARER EXPECTATIONS MEAN BETTER OUTCOMES

When you communicate clear expectations, your team will work together on a shared goal. They'll feel motivated by clear goals, responsibilities, and deliverables. It may sound simple, but managing expectations properly is the easiest way to go from merely getting the work done to excelling in every aspect of our work.

What I have attempted to do in this chapter is to highlight the importance of setting your expectations accurately and inclusively. I have seen and felt the results of falling short of doing this well but thankfully learnt from the experience. Hopefully, if you are reading this ahead of being that person carrying the responsibility, you do not have to fall foul of my mistakes.

Walk in your team's shoes, and set them up for success, and you will enjoy success across all aspects of your work and projects. Do this consistently, and you will always be surrounded by the best people because you will have prepared them to be so.

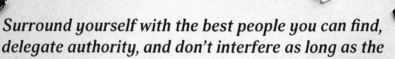

Surround yourself with the best people you can find, delegate authority, and don't interfere as long as the policy you've decided upon is being carried out.

Ronald Regan, President of the United States of America

Now that we've considered how to effectively communicate the mission to the team, let's take a look at what goals look like.

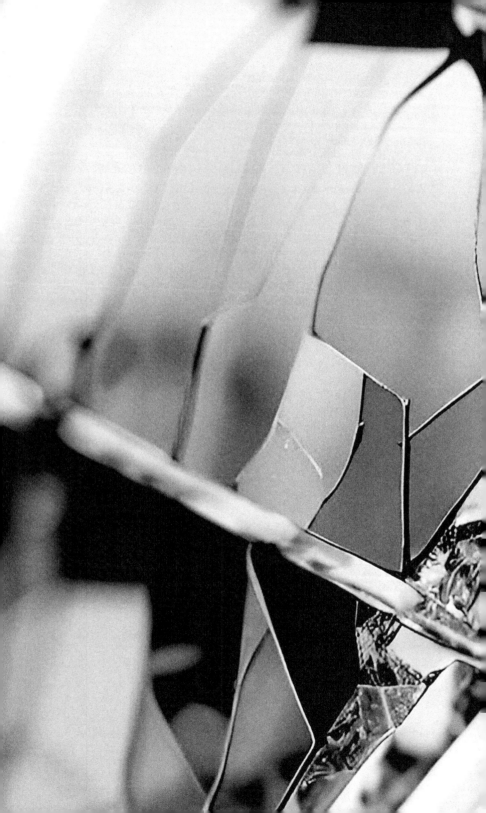

Going for Gold

It was pitch black, and the helicopter was bouncing around in the wind and rain as we neared the landing site. The noise was so loud that talking or shouting to my men was pointless, so I gave the hand signal that we would be landing in one minute. The loadmaster readied us and as he slid the door open, letting in the sound of the rotors chopping the air and the rush of the wash of the blades, the all-pervading noise in the cabin became ten times louder.

ENTERING THE ZONE

We scrambled to get out of the heli (Army slang for helicopter) with our kit and into an all-round defence formation before it lifted off, leaving us in the very wet, dark Welsh mountains. *Which way do I go now?* This is a question I had asked myself many times and in various situations, but this time was different because of the weight of expectation on my shoulders.

I was lying there, soaked to the skin, with 80 pounds (over 36 kilograms) of kit on my back, 65 kilometres or so ahead of me, and my section of infantry soldiers to take with me—all highly trained but looking to me for the next move. *Alright, Steve. We have trained for this, and you are ready to lead these men. Get up and take the first step, and the rest will fall into place.*

PARALYSIS BY ANALYSIS

We have all been in a place or a situation that we did not engineer or want to find ourselves in, right? You will have been at a junction where you didn't know which way to turn—*Do I turn left, take the right or give up?*—but there is nothing worse than being hit with paralysis by analysis, when the sheer volume of information, fear and/or choice renders you incapable of deciding or taking action.

Paralysis by analysis is not the state to be in as a highly-trained soldier or officer of the British Army. That's why we train to never have to face this in battle. Countless exercises, drill sessions, and scenario-planning sessions can all but irradicate this risk, but fear is another beast entirely and takes a different resolve to tame. On that wintry night in Wales, I needed to get us moving and trust that my plan and the enormous amount of work we had done as a team would kick in and our collective mindset would settle into the zone quickly.

That's the thing about Army training. We train to act as one unit, whether there are only a few of us or dozens. Every soldier understands the goal and the part they need to play to ensure we achieve it. Once the plan is made and the order is issued, everyone works as a team and the machine is activated. We think and behave as one unit, but every person needs to have the power to think and act independently if the situation requires it.

So, what the hell was I doing face-down in vegetation deep in the Welsh mountains in the dead of the night?

THE CAMBRIAN PATROL

I was a young lieutenant platoon commander on an operational tour of Northern Ireland when I got the call from my commanding officer to lead the battalion's Cambrian Patrol team, an honour indeed but one that you accept with caution as the stakes are high.

The Cambrian Patrol is the British Army's toughest infantry skills competition. It runs once a year and attracts competitors from the best armies in the world. As you'd expect for an event that is internationally recognised for its toughness, it takes place in the depths of the Welsh mountains and, yes, in the middle of winter! It is considered quite the achievement to complete this gruelling competition with all of your men, and to win one of the bronze, silver or gold awards up for grabs is something that battalion legends are made of.

DAVID JACKSON—A LEGEND IN THE RANKS

One such legend in my battalion was David Jackson. In my eyes, he was one of the most impressive officers that I had ever met, and indeed, I looked up to him and his example as an officer on every level. He was physically strong, as mentally sharp as a lance, and had his shit together in every way. More than that, he also happened to be a great bloke and genuinely wanted us junior officers to do well.

David had led the last Cambrian team from my battalion, and as you may have guessed, he came back with a gold—a fucking gold medal from the Cambrian Patrol. You can imagine what was going through my mind as I was standing in front of my commanding officer as he extolled the virtues of my taking on the custodianship of our battalion's Cambrian Patrol future. If I am attracted to anything, it's the possibility of the challenge of tackling big stuff, and this was big stuff—get it right, and I would be cementing my legendary status; get it wrong, and you can work that out for yourself.

Self-belief is what made it easy for me to accept this challenge. I was calm because I knew I could do this. During my specialist infantry training after Sandhurst, I was awarded a pass with distinction, and that was all the affirmation I needed to know my capabilities, but this time, I needed to find a band of brothers from which I would have to select a team of seven (plus reserves) who shared that belief in themselves and belief in the team that we would form.

SOURCING THE BEST OF THE BEST

Anything less than gold would not do, so I was going to have to be ruthless in the selection of the team and those who would help with the preparation. This approach seems harsh and potentially cold, and it is not one that I employ day to day (not rigorously anyway), but the challenge that lay ahead was significant. It would have been cruel to select someone who I knew was not strong enough for what we would be facing on those hills. As a leader, never invite failure, especially for others.

I was given the support of the Training Wing Team (the squad of specialist training personnel who deliver training across the Army) to train us, so theoretically all we needed to do was get on with the programme laid down for us. I spoke to the training team in advance to see the programme and to reassure myself that we were about to put our trust in the right hands. I am not a control freak, but I like to have a degree of control in any situation where I am leading, not necessarily of all the detail but the strategic direction of travel and the plan that supports us getting there.

We followed a thorough three-day selection process and managed to pull together a team of nine. That meant we only had one in reserve when we would have preferred four because I knew the training to come would likely be too much for some. There was no point taking people on just to make up the numbers. Every member of the team, including anyone in reserve, would need to have high levels of resilience, mental strength, physical fitness, and a positive mental attitude for us to succeed.

As luck would have it, two members of the previous gold-winning team made the selection, and their experience and stories of how they cracked the level of performance that is needed to land a gold would prove to be invaluable, helping us all prepare in the best possible way for what lay ahead.

CEMENTING THE TEAM—LEARNING TO BE TOGETHER

Our first two weeks were all about learning to be together, one of the other pillars of structure identified by Jacques Delors. The competition was only eight weeks away, so we deployed to Wales to live, train, eat and socialise together to help us to bond as a team as quickly as possible. Over that fortnight, we would also be learning to do (Delors again), learning how to think and act as elite infantry soldiers across terrain that has broken many a soldier—the same terrain that the SAS use for their selection process.

Do you know when something does not feel right? Well, day one with the training wing staff in Wales was one of those situations for me. Quite frankly, it was too easy. I was expecting to be pushed to breaking point, physically and in the classroom. I had visions of reporting to the playing fields at 0500 hours for bear crawling lengths at a time, press-ups, fireman's lifts, running circuits of the pitch, and burpees, with showering, shaving, eating and a bit of sleep in between sessions. The reality was not even close, and I was left with the impression that training was going to be a mix of standard physical training and classroom sessions. As I looked out of the classroom window and took in the sight of the imposing, intimidating, wild Welsh mountains, I knew that's where we needed to be. Standard physical training wouldn't be enough!

TRAIN HARD, FIGHT EASY

Learning in the classroom has its place, and I'm sure we could expect to be pushed in the gym, but we had control of those conditions. We wouldn't have anywhere near the same level of control out there in the wilderness. Being physically fit and trained in a controlled environment would not be enough for what we were up against.

Train hard, fight easy is a phrase you'll often see in boxing gyms. If you want to succeed in a physically challenging environment, you have to put yourself through more than you expect to face in the competition. Soldiers call it getting beasted— which means being pushed to one's limits mentally and physically—but we needed to be stretched in the right way. Boxers put in hundreds of hours in the ring when preparing for a fight. Training hard for us surely had to mean spending at least four hours every day in the mountains. After all, they were right there on our doorstep.

You can only fight the way you practise.

Miyamoto Musashi, *The Book of Five Rings*

I spoke to my second-in-command, Andy, about my unease with the situation and agreed to see how the week went before I acted. The week passed slowly, and the situation did not change, so I approached the colour sergeant in charge of training and told him that it was off-pace and not fit for what we needed. He hit the roof, and I mean completely lost his shit.

TAKING CHARGE

If you've served in the armed forces, you will already know about the contempt shown to officers while they earn their wings, especially by the senior non-commissioned officers (SNCOs). Telling the colour sergeant his training regime was not up to scratch could only go one way—due south! For me to even consider escalating things shows how convinced I was that something had to change. It was not a decision I took lightly.

He was not up to the job, I was on the hook for delivering on this competition, and I had seven men who needed me to be their leader, and that meant action. Unsurprisingly, the colour sergeant had no intention of budging on the issue, so the solution was easy: I ordered him to stand down and told him that I would be taking over the training for the remainder of our time in Wales. This proved to be a game-changer.

On return to our home barracks, I reported what had happened to my commanding officer and asked for all responsibility for training the team to be handed over to me. Things have to be done the right way in the Army, and while I had the authority to take over from the colour sergeant, I wanted to ensure he was not reinstated.

My commander agreed, but it caused a major falling-out across the battalion, especially with the training wing and the colour sergeant who had effectively been sacked by a young officer. The colour sergeant hated me and wanted me and my team to fail. Later, I would use this hatred to drive the motivation of the men on the hills, so he did me a favour.

KNOW WHEN TO ACT

The point here is that when it is not good enough, it is not good enough, and action must be taken. We nearly missed an opportunity in Wales, so I was not about to miss another. I would train the team, but we would do it together systematically, using all our skills collaboratively.

The first step was to plan out the next six weeks and to gain full buy-in from every member of the team. Remember the lessons learnt in the last chapter. Billy needs to know why he must keep up! The whole team agreed to a set of behaviours, an unwritten contract, which covered who would do what, what standards we expected from each other, how we would continually test ourselves in preparation, and how we would measure progress along the way.

DICED

Nothing was off the table. I used a simple model to guide our discussion and make sure that we were all on the same page. DICED would become our handrail:

- Define **the mission**—what does the end goal look like? Cambrian gold in this instance!
- Important—it must be equally important for every member of the team, not just the leader. That full buy-in ensured that we fought for every breath while preparing for and during the competition.
- Can-do attitude—mindset is everything. An unshakeable belief was vital to achieving our goal. We had the skills, we would develop and test the fitness levels needed, and we'd support each other all the way.
- Expectation—expect success. We expected gold, so we were always focused. Expectations affect the process. How does

every aspect of this performance, action or learning help us on the journey, and how do we measure those variables? If you can't measure it, you can't improve it!

- **D**eserved—recognise that you are as entitled to success as the next person. All you have to do is to put the work in. We deserved the success that our hard work would bring.

Strong belief is vital to achieving our goals in life. What do you believe you can achieve, and what will you do to accomplish it? If we believe that we can fly and simply jump from a plane at 10,000 feet, we are more likely to die trying or be locked away for our safety and that of others. Belief without a realistic plan and a commitment to taking effective action is nothing more than an empty opinion. But to believe in what the collective efforts of a well-drilled and emotionally connected team can deliver is part of the contract that any successful team signs up for, and by the end of our short six weeks together, that is what we had. Every one of us believed we could win, and we were going to do whatever it would take to make that happen. This team was going to achieve amazing things that none of us could do on our own.

OPERATION CAMBRIAN

For the strength of the pack
is the wolf,
and the strength of the wolf
is the pack.

Rudyard Kipling—The Jungle Book

Alright, Steve. We have trained for this, and you are ready to lead these men. Get up and take the first step. I reminded myself of our DICED commitment, and off we went.

The next 42 hours were tough, very tough; we hit problems, we each had low points and needed each other, but we all had each other. One big issue cropped up around 40 kilometres in when my radio operator, who was carrying the equipment we needed to send our situation reps (situation reports) to headquarters, picked up an injury. If we didn't finish as a team, with all eight men, we couldn't win the gold.

To keep my radio guy going, I took his radio kit in my pack. As part of our strategy to minimise the risk of injuries, we carefully distributed all our equipment equally across the whole team, so that no one was carrying more than the other. This meant that we each started with about 82 pounds, over 37 kilograms, or six-stone-worth of kit in our packs plus our helmets, which had to be worn, and our rifles. The radio kit was about twenty pounds (around nine kilograms) in total, so my pack was about to get an extra stone and a half, which was a stretch, but I was strong; however, what became a greater challenge was that it didn't fit in my pack and sat tall, poking out at the top and pushing my neck and head forward. This was so uncomfortable, it made me angry, and perhaps that's what kept me going, that and my resolve to get us all over the line. We were in this together, so we cracked on, trial after trial, kilometre after kilometre, all eight of us determined that the gold would not allude us while we had answers to situations.

On the final approach to the last trial that we would face before crossing the finishing line, I sensed something was not right. I felt that we should be further on than we were. You learn to trust your instincts and intuition. If you feel it, it is almost certainly real. I had been navigating with nearly eight stone on my back, soaking wet, and like everyone else, knackered after 55 kilometres or so.

The weight was one thing, but the pressing on my neck eventually got to me, affecting my concentration, and I failed to stop for a navigation check at a critical part of the journey. I had taken us down the wrong path! *Fuck. What do I do now? I have to stop and admit to everyone that I have cocked up here and that we need to go to ground to allow me to reset.*

I put the men into their sleeping bags in the wood line (the edge of a wooded area of trees) to warm up and rest while I regained my composure and worked out how to pull this situation back from the precipice. Have you ever been in a situation that is so delicate that even the slightest movement to the left or right could be catastrophic? This was it. Various thoughts were running through my head at once—the men, the effort, what that prick of a colour sergeant would think if we arrived home with nothing, my ego (more pride really as I am not an egotistical person, not at all), and what my commanding officer would think, having investing so much trust in me to get the job done.

OODA

In Army Staff College, we were introduced to a decision-making cycle called the OODA loop, which was created by the US military strategist Colonel John R. Boyd. In his seminal paper, 'Destruction and Creation', he proposed a theory that was directly applicable to fast-changing environments, and the OODA loop was born.

OODA stands for observe, orientate, decide, and act. The loop is easy to learn and apply, and it's something I have found very useful in my military and business careers. Once, I had the pleasure of teaching it to a group of US officers while on exercise with them. To my amusement, they had never heard of it but were, of course, very pleased to learn that it was one of their own who created it.

We were lost, and it was on me to get us back on track. I had to think fast because the longer those men stayed in their warm sleeping bags, the harder it would be to get them going again. This is precisely the kind of situation where OODA can help.

OBSERVE

This is about collecting the data. *What is the situation?* We were lost and tired, but I knew we were close because of the amount of terrain we had already covered. Fortunately, we hadn't strayed too far from the navigation checkpoint we had missed. I was accountable to my team, so I admitted my mistake quickly and took ownership of the situation. It would not take long to get a fix on where we were and where we needed to get back to.

ORIENTATE

This is the analysis. I needed to get back to the last known point where I knew our position and which way we should be going. *What are my options? Give up, track back to that last known checkpoint as a team, or go it alone to that point so that the men can rest and not be punished for my mistake.*

DECIDE

After observation of the situation and analysis of the options, it's time to make choice. I did and decided that I would track back myself to test my hypothesis of where I believed I had gone wrong. The men would take turns resting in the warmth of their sleeping bags for fifteen minutes at a time. I could not risk them getting into a deep sleep. We had been without sleep for over 40 hours and burnt calories like a steam engine burning coal. Allowing them to fall into a deep sleep now only to wake them up and expect them to continue would mess them up physically at best and break their spirit at worst. I took responsibility, made the decision, and off I went, back from where we'd come. Vitally, per DICED, I still believed that I could turn this around. My expectation had not been knocked off course, just my map reading and only temporarily!

ACT

I was off at pace. I left my pack with the men, taking only my webbing and rifle (you never leave your rifle more than one arm's length from you) and jogged back. It was not long before I was at the point where I thought I had made my error, and it was not that far from where I had left the men. I was on the tree line with my map when I saw one of the competition staff members arrive at the corner of the woods opposite me. I marched over to him as if I had intended it all along.

'McNally checking in, Corporal. ' I said, with all the energy and enthusiasm of a substitute player running onto the pitch of a soccer game after being stuck on the bench for 80 minutes.

'What's your situation?' he asked.

I told him that I'd tactically placed my men further down the track so I could check in with him and give them a chance to rest. He bought it, and it turned out quite well for us.

'OK, McNally. Go get your men, and bring them back here. I'll take you to the final trial.'

Phew!

'Thank you, Corporal. I'll be back within the hour.'

Now, we're talking. I had fucked up but just slightly, and victory was within our grasp.

When I got back to the men, they were as knackered as I'd expected them to be, and it took a bit of a Churchill 'On the beaches' speech to persuade them that getting out of their snug sleeping bags and putting those heavy packs on their backs was a great idea. They did it, though, and in the spirit of DICED, they reminded each other that we deserved to finish the competition together as a complete team.

JOB DONE

We crossed the finish line together, and what followed was amazing. Completing the mission was already a glorious feeling but to find out that we'd won gold and were the highest-scoring team that year—out of some one hundred and fifteen teams from across the British Army and other forces internationally—was something that none of us will ever forget.

By getting rid of those charged with preparing us, we took a risk, but we had bonded through our adherence to DICED, held each other accountable, laughed together, suffered together, and more than anything else, always been there for each other.

Our team was tight from the beginning, and our experience in the Welsh mountains only made us all closer. I'd watched them grow over what amounted to a very short period, and it was even more rewarding to see that every single one of them went on to enjoy accelerated career success. I hope that our adventure together helped them to achieve that.

It is rare in life to be tested so intensely on so many levels within such a brief timeframe, but what it taught me is that if you are bold, set a vision that everyone can see and articulate, take responsibility for the delivery, and lead in a manner that your team would want to be led, you can achieve exceptional results. We had the wildest celebratory party in Blackpool, England, on the way home, but that's another story!

DREAM BIG

Do not be worried about setting big crazy goals! Go for gold even if only metaphorically—visualise it, live the feeling of success as if you already have it, and thank the universe for giving it to you. We do not sit and dwell on the rain outside our windows. At least, you don't if, like me, you live in Northern Ireland. If you did, you would have an awful time of it. Yes, it might disrupt your plans a little, but we can just adapt, and do a bit of OODA looping on it. *It's pissing it down. Will it kill me? No. Can I go out? Yes, but I will have to get wrapped up. Do I have to go out? No. What options do I have? Stay in, visit the gym, or take a stroll in the park with wellies and an umbrella if I'm feeling adventurous. Gym, it is*—kit packed, car keys, coat on, and action!

Don't forget the principles of DICED. Suppose you were constantly worried about how your dog behaved or how your children were going to turn out. Stop worrying, and focus on doing something about it (define the mission). Train the dog, and spend time with your children. Give everything to the things that are worthy of your investment (important), and trust that you have done a good job (can-do attitude and expectation). Don't be the person who fails to achieve their potential because they feel that they don't deserve it.

A very good friend of mine David Meade, who you will hear more about later, once told me a story about the time he told his mum he had written a pitch for a television show. 'What if you don't get it?' she asked. David's response?

'What if I do?'

That's one of my favourite true stories, and in case you're wondering, yes, he got the thumbs-up for his television show.

CHALLENGES ARE THE STUFF OF GROWTH

I lost my father early in my life, but I was determined not to let that hinder me from pursuing the abundant opportunities that awaited me. Do not let your circumstances define you, and do not dwell on what you cannot control. Focus on what you can control. The struggle against circumstances can, if embraced, propel us to a new level of functioning, pushing us to stay present with the endless possibilities available to us. The size and scope of our challenges often determine how much potential there is for growth and success from the experience. Ambitious goal setting is therefore a recipe for self-development.

Each to their own. One person's nemesis is another's stroll in the park. You do not need to throw eight stones on your back and trek for 60 kilometres across crazy mountain terrain as I did. That goal was meant for me. You have to find your way. It might be taking a course at your local college, committing to a daily walk with your friend, or just being more present for your loved ones.

If we look upon our obstacles as opportunities that we can use to our advantage by helping us build our better selves, we will attract successes, and no matter how small they appear, the cumulative effect will be a more fulfilled, happier, and productive life.

In the next chapter, we'll be considering the power of mindset and how to rewire our thinking to achieve more. For the moment, consider this:

What gold will you go for now?

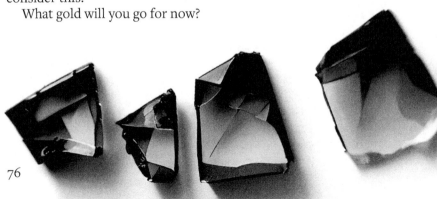

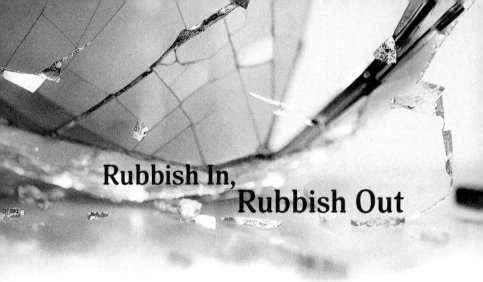

Rubbish In, Rubbish Out

It was a typical hot and sweaty wet-season night in Freetown, Sierra Leone, and I was in the town's most welcoming bar for squaddies. Even during the darkest times, Paddy's was a safe place for the international community to go and enjoy a drink and something to eat, but I wasn't having a good time. A guy called Tim, one of my team whom I had been having a bit of an issue with, was drinking in the same bar, and I'd made up my mind to say something.

I leaned into him: 'Tim, the only way we are going to sort this out is in the backyard. You and I are going to go out there to slug this out the old-fashioned way. The person who comes back inside gets to do things their way!'

Tim was visibly shocked that an officer would suggest a straightener as a resolution. As a seasoned non-commissioned officer, I didn't expect him to be too concerned about the prospect of a bare-knuckle fight, and I thought he'd feel confident that he could sort me out without too much difficulty. He probably thought I'd back down before we got outside, but there was no chance of that, not with this boy. 'Let's go, Tim. I don't want my beer to get warm.' I wasn't happy, and I needed to act. It was that simple. I'd rather risk a beating trying to change the situation than accept things as they were.

You might be wondering why I had a beef with Tim and how it had escalated to the point that I was prepared to have a fistfight.

THE INTERNATIONAL MILITARY
ASSISTANCE AND TRAINING TEAM

Three weeks earlier, I arrived in Sierra Leone as part of the International Military Assistance and Training Team (IMATT) to lead the infantry training of a batch of officer cadets and soldiers. I was there to join an established team to help them with a programme that had already been designed and approved. They needed an officer with suitable experience in infantry skills facilitation to oversee delivery.

Shortly after landing, I grabbed a heli to our main base where I got into military kit, packed a day sack (backpack for military kit), and jumped in a waiting Land Rover Defender. As soon as I arrived at the exercise area, I had a strong sense that things were not right. Call it instinct, or call it experience, but something felt off. I approached one of the colour sergeants (senior ranks). 'Colour, take me to see the troops.'

It was pouring down, which was to be expected in the deep jungle in the wet season. There is no point in wearing waterproof kit in these conditions. You can't avoid getting wet, but you make sure you have a dry set of kit ready for when you find shelter and can rest. In these conditions, however, you need to admin yourself (Army-speak for taking care of yourself) diligently; otherwise, you will go man down (get injured or just fall apart).

A JUNGLE RIDE

We were 40 minutes into our patrol, out to see around three hundred troops, whom I was expecting to find in several company harbours, clearly marked out in a standard triangle formation and manned at the corners for security. Harbours are military formations of up to 80 soldiers, set up when operations are halted for a while.

Something about the colour sergeant who was guiding me to the soldiers prompted me to ask if he was all right. 'Yes, Sir,' came the reply. *Okay, if you're happy, I'm happy*, I thought to myself. 'How long, now, until we reach the harbour, Colour?'

'Twenty minutes, Sir.'

Hmm. Something didn't feel right. They should not be so far away from the exercise base, so I wasn't surprised when, around twenty minutes later, we were wetter, and there was still no sign of the troops.

'Colour, are you lost?'

This question, from an officer who had just arrived, would have felt like a hot knife to the heart for the colour; however, he didn't know me, and I would rather deal with the issue than focus on the mistake. I was there to lead, not to break the team by embarrassing them for an error that was easy to make considering the conditions and the challenge of navigating in the jungle.

'I am, Sir.'

I appreciated him coming clean.

'Okay, we can deal with that. Let's go back to the last point that you know you can pinpoint on the map.' A look of relief flashed across the colour's face as the tension that had been building up over the last thirty minutes or so lifted. He'd been spared a bollocking and been given a plan of action.

A SOGGY SHIT SHOW

Within half-an-hour, we found the troops, although, at first glance, I almost wished we hadn't. They were in what we call in military terms shite order! Their stuff was strewn all over the place and getting soaked because they hadn't set up an overhead cover to provide a dry area for administration. It was a terrible harbour, the worst I had ever seen, but I didn't say anything about it to the colour sergeant; instead, I asked him to take me to the exercise HQ (headquarters). I needed to meet the boss, Lieutenant Colonel Mike.

As soon as I spotted the chief, it was immediately clear why everything was in disarray. He was asleep on a bench, while all around us was chaos. I woke him and introduced myself as his new infantry training officer (ITO). His first words were 'What do you think so far?' followed by 'We are expecting the head of the mission to visit this evening.' *Yikes!* This train wreck did not need another set of eyes on it.

The head of our IMATT team was Colonel Matt O'Hanlon, and, luckily, I had worked for him before, when he was a commanding officer of my battalion. I'd been his operations officer on an operational tour in Northern Ireland. The Army runs a very strict chain of command and going above the head of a superior officer can easily put their nose out of joint; however, my boss was not aware that I had worked with the colonel, so, with the right approach, I could make sure Colonel Matt didn't hit the roof, without Lieutenant Colonel Mike ever having to know.

The colonel was a fair but very firm officer who expected high standards, but I had no issue with that; to this day, I rate him as one of the most inspiring officers I have ever worked with and for.

As soon as he arrived, I grabbed him at his vehicle and disclosed that this place and the exercise were not in good order but that I would sort it; I also explained that, for me to do that, I would need him not to kick off immediately and to tell the team that he would be holding me responsible for all aspects of the training design and delivery from that point forward. By transferring responsibility from them to me, I hoped to get the rest of the team behind me as friendly forces, not the enemy within.

Once I'd finished briefing him on the situation, I took him on a quick tour to show him how disorganised things were and to explain what my next steps were going to be. He wasn't happy when he left, but he was content that there was a plan and, more importantly, the right person was in place to execute it.

RUBBISH OUT

Over the next 48 hours, I dissected the training plan that had been put together for the next six months for this cohort of soldiers and officers, and I concluded that it was fundamentally wrong. It was fixable except for the fact that it had been produced by a so-called training design expert called Tim, the same Tim whom I ended up inviting for a fight. I was going to have to convince him and the boss that we needed to go back to the drawing board. This proved to be quite the challenge.

My understanding of why Tim had arrived at his design was simple: He was not an infantry officer, had never been deployed on an operational tour where he had to fight. and, lastly, he didn't care. He didn't care about the end game for these soldiers, which was the future security of their country. I did. Having lived in Northern Ireland during The Troubles, I knew what it was like to not have security in my country.

These three hundred soldiers and officers were the first to be openly recruited from the local population of Sierra Leone, and they had a real chance to change the outcomes for their country—no more military coups and no more war. We had the opportunity to bring about that stability by training them effectively. It was meaningful, worthwhile work that we could be proud of—a privilege.

I needed to build a culture for tomorrow into the training plan to ensure these soldiers could maintain stability for years to come, a culture of service before self, country as community, and personal responsibility; I wanted to develop a team of people who would do the right thing even when they thought no one was watching.

It was a case of going back to basics and designing a programme built on the practical principles of doing. There had to be an element of classroom learning, but, if these men and women were going to be the anchor of security in their homeland, they were going to need practical experience in the field to develop the required skills.

The training they had already received was, quite frankly, rubbish. We needed to throw that away and start again, but a change in the training plan wasn't going to be enough. My colleagues also needed to change their attitudes and their approach. I needed them to care as much as I did, and they didn't. They couldn't see the point, and neither could my boss. It was as though, from their perspective, they'd been deployed to a jungle on another continent to tick a box by delivering training for the sake of it, and they didn't believe their work could make a difference.

WHAT CHANGED?

Two weeks in, we were back on exercise with the troops but this time, we were doing it my way. I built an exercise HQ for all my staff that was only five minutes from where the troops were deployed in a properly formed harbour with shelter. They had tasks to perform where we could see them, and they knew that we cared.

Colonel Mike insisted that he did not want to stay in the HQ that I had built. I tried to reason with him: 'But, Sir, this is where you need to be as the commanding officer, in the ops room!' He wasn't interested, however, because he wanted to sleep in a hammock, outside of the HQ, in an old colonial building that was partly covered by jungle; he thought this would be fun. Despite my best efforts to warn him that, firstly, he would be on his own and, secondly, the building was not robust enough to provide a suitable anchor for the hammock, he went ahead anyway. Who was I to come between a lieutenant colonel and his sense of fun?

Just after three in the morning, I heard an almighty crash followed by a scream that was nearly as loud. I grabbed my kit and rifle and ran to where I thought the noise had come from. Sure enough, the walls of the house had collapsed on the boss. I scrambled the staff; we extracted him from the rubble and contacted our main HQ to alert them that we had a casualty.

It turned out that his injuries were so serious, with a fractured pelvis for a start, he could not be treated in Sierra Leone and had to be flown to England on an RAF plane. How embarrassing must it have been to fly back from an area of conflict not because of injuries sustained while engaging with enemy forces but because of a fall from a hammock? I guess that's the price of fun. Play stupid games, win stupid prizes.

I became the boss, and although I would never wish Lieutenant Colonel Mike's injuries on anyone, his accident cleared the way for me to get on with the job unencumbered by politics. The only other obstacle was Tim, but fortunately for me, he didn't have the balls to let my drink get warm that night in Paddy's, so he was out of the picture as well.

When I arrived in Sierra Leone, the team had been established for a while, and it was clear that the culture was self-serving and not driven by the greater purpose; to my mind, that purpose was to empower these people to help themselves to avoid further civil war and bring an end to the accompanying atrocities that were being perpetrated at that time.

Cultures evolve whether you want them to or not, so you might as well take control of the process and strive to grow a culture that fits and supports your purpose—the Why, the How, and the what will follow. With Colonel Mike and Tim out of the way, I seized the opportunity to grow the culture of tomorrow. Rubbish out; start afresh.

Over the next six months, I spent every day with the soldiers and officers and hope the example I set for them served as a fair reflection of the doctrine I wanted them to adopt once I had left. While I cannot and would not try to claim that my time in Sierra Leone is the reason that the country has not returned to its violent past, I like to think that my work there made a positive contribution to the current stable situation. My experience in Sierra Leone has had a significant impact on me, and I will return to that later.

CHANGE THE STORY, CHANGE YOUR LIFE

If you cast your mind back to one of the earlier chapters, you might remember this:

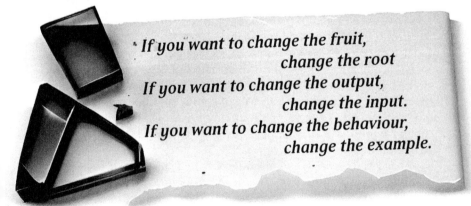

> If you want to change the fruit,
> change the root
> If you want to change the output,
> change the input.
> If you want to change the behaviour,
> change the example.

I was born into a very ordinary, working-class environment, although I use working-class loosely as there was often more unemployment than employment. Some of what I experienced with the different men that arrived at our home after my father had died may have been an attempt to stave off the financial impact of poverty, but it was not just money that impacted us. It was the lack of emotional investment—of being there, stepping in, filling the gaps that our father would have filled, and talking about what we could achieve.

Some of this lack may have been a reflection of the challenging Northern Irish economy at the time; The Troubles brought more issues to the country than the violence we saw in the streets or on the nightly television news. I guess the perceived lack of opportunity and the compound effect of telling ourselves that we were not meant for more became a self-fulfilling prophecy; even if opportunities were there, we were unlikely to seek them out or grab them.

My immediate family did not consider or even talk about how we might break the cycle. That was my rubbish in—the example to follow, the attitude to inherit, and the expectation that I should accept my lot just as the rest of my family did. Not me; I was determined to change the fruit, the output, and the behaviours.

If you can't see it, you can't be it.

Marianne Elliot ,
British Film Director

Marianne Elliot's not wrong. Everything began to change when I started working in the chippy with Keith because, through his example, I could see it, and I was bloody well going to be it! He aimed for the stars in the business world, and he owned everything he did. I believe we all have a personal responsibility to leave things in a better state than we found them. It is our responsibility as humans, and that applies to everyone, but parents have an even greater

83

responsibility. We must strive to bring our children up in a way that prevents them from having to undo the damage caused by our parenting. Let's not add to the 'rubbish in' for the next generation. How can we be free of this construct? How do we break the cycle and change the input for the better?

BREAKING THE CYCLE

If we want to escape the impact of rubbish in and the inevitable rubbish out, we must first become conscious of it. This syndrome is not symptom-free, and those symptoms have an impact, so we start by looking for evidence of that impact—our results and our mental and physical health. Once we are aware of the impact, we can begin to shine a light on the symptoms—the assumptions, beliefs and behaviours that have helped to create our outcomes. To turn things around, we need to build a new story where we get to be the star rather than a bystander or non-speaking extra.

Life is a journey, so it helps to know where we are heading or at least roughly where we want to get to. Once we have defined the goal and mapped out the steps we need to take to get there, these steps become the building blocks of our new story. They allow us to reflect, measure progress and ensure that we remain aligned with our purpose. Of course, we must consider the future at the planning stage, but once the new story begins, we have to operate in the present, free from the impact of any negative thoughts, emotions, or distractions.

I don't claim to be an expert on the psychology of rewriting the script, but many books have been written on the topic for those who want to explore the subject further. What I can share are the tools that have worked for me on my journey.

If I had surrendered to the story of my childhood, allowed my working-class background to define me, accepted that I was destined to remain on the side of the Protestants or Catholics, loved my job in the chippy enough to stay, married my first serious girlfriend, and swam in my little pond for the rest of my life, I would not have become the man I am today.

I am grateful for the life I have had and the experiences that I have gained along the way, some hard fought for, some joyous, and many life-changing, and I hope that by sharing these with others, I can help change at least one life for the better.

TAKE TIME TO GET TO KNOW YOURSELF, WARTS AND ALL!

Emotional self-awareness is the foundation from which we can build our emotional intelligence. We can't change what we don't recognise, so investing time to look inwards will pay dividends for you and everyone around you. A breakthrough moment for me was recognising my triggers, the things that annoyed me and at times provoked a negative response. The goal was not to find a way to avoid those triggers but to change my response to them. Feeling angry doesn't have to lead to aggressive behaviour.

GET A MENTOR, COACH OR BOTH

I have used both and get great value from the conversations I have with them. If you are going to use them, it is important to recognise the difference between a mentor and a coach and to know what you want to get from each. An appropriate mentor will have experience in the journey you are exploring, and they can use that to guide you on how to navigate yours. A coach, however, doesn't need to know anything about your area of expertise. They will ask smart questions to help you to identify some of those symptoms we spoke about earlier—the self-limiting beliefs and other barriers we create to hold us back.

I look up to my mentor, and they help me to solve difficult problems that they have often already encountered or have superior knowledge of. My coach and I have a different relationship, based on listening and helping me to discover the solutions for the challenges we discuss. If I know the answers, the coach will help me to draw them out. If that doesn't work, my mentor will give me the solution I am looking for.

NAIL FIRST IMPRESSIONS

First encounters are always scary moments, especially if, like me, you are an introvert who has to expend personal currency with every interaction. We need to nail it fast so that we have some balance left in the account. Planning is a game-changer.

Have your introduction ready; if you think you may struggle to kick off a conversation, use WTF—work, travel and fun—as anyone you speak to will have done some of that recently and will usually be only too happy to share a story.

Do your research and dress for the occasion. If you have never seen the 1996 *Only Fools and Horses* Christmas special, 'Villains and Heroes', take a look on YouTube, and you will see a perfect example of why it is important to dress for the day!

TELL GREAT STORIES

Learn to tell stories. Yes, *learn*! This is a skill that is within the grasp of us all. How have all the great entrepreneurs, presidents and leaders of the world got to where they are? They told powerful stories, stories that engaged their audiences at an emotional level. Stories can be built and framed or reframed in a way that talks directly to your audience or indeed to us—the stories we tell ourselves can be transformative (data in).

Stories bring words to life and deliver an experience; they illuminate and inspire. Think of the last time you were shown a PowerPoint slide. Can you remember what the text said? You probably can't, right, but if I ask you to think of a story that you heard as a child, I guarantee you will recall plenty of detail without trying too hard. Stories become etched in our psyches and stay with us for decades.

WORK WELL WITH OTHERS

Diverse teams produce better results. This is a proven fact, so build a team around you or be the best team member you can be. The value of collective intelligence should never be underestimated and must always be leveraged to achieve great results. In the teams that I have been fortunate to be a part of, some of which have been awarded gold medals for their performance, I have never been more capable or intelligent than the team—never! Can I suggest that no one ever has? Even if you're the smartest in the room, we all have blind spots, and we are limited by experience. The hive mind will have greatly more experience and a wider perspective.

LET IT GO

Worry never robs tomorrow of its sorrow; it only saps today of its joy.

Leo Buscaglia, *Motivational Speaker and Writer*

When something unfortunate happens, try to put it in perspective. It is unlikely to be the end of the world and will almost certainly have a solution, especially if you have the collective intelligence of a team of trusted colleagues, a mentor or a coach. Reframe it and deal with it.

ALWAYS LOOK FOR GROWTH

Why should you adopt a growth mindset? Simply put, the opposite of growth shows us why. If our mindsets are fixed, it is only a matter of time before the wind, tide, or time erodes us from existence because we cannot stop the outside world from changing. We must adapt to keep up. Keep moving and learning and stay with the pack. Lifelong learners live longer.

I am very much a work in progress, but I have come to recognise rubbish in before it can get a chance to set up camp, ensuring that it doesn't lead to rubbish out. I have learnt to reframe my story and build a much more productive one for myself. That is not to say that I do not painfully remember the challenges that I have faced, but I have a safe place for these memories now; they are in a museum in the back of my mind where, for a small fee, I can view them but leave behind when I am getting on with life.

The seven tips I have shared here are just a few of the many tools that are available to all of us. I have used these and more to get me to the place I am today, and I will continue to do so. Possibly the most important tool of all is the growth mindset because that will ensure you find the tools you need to adapt to the ever-changing conditions you find yourself in while preparing for the road ahead. Adopt a growth mindset, and you can be sure that growth will find you.

In the next chapter, we will explore other tools that can help us to succeed in life and business while looking at some of the tools we've already covered in more detail.

Building
Blockbuster Teams

The English comedian, actor, writer and presenter, Tom Allen, known for hosting *The Apprentice: You're Fired* and co-hosting *Cooking with the Stars* as well as winning the *So You Think You're Funny* contest in 2005, is a particular favourite of mine. His quick-witted humour never fails to make me laugh, and I admire the cut of his suit, the perfectly put-together shirt and tie combinations, and more than anything, his perfectly groomed head! Yes, 'perfectly groomed head,' I said; Tom is a fellow follically challenged gentleman who wears it fabulously.

Why have I opened this chapter with a declaration of my admiration for Tom? Because any mention of him brings back a very special memory. I will never forget his words on a dark wintry evening in November 2021, when I was with my work teammates in London to attend the Learning Technologies Awards, the equivalent of the Oscars in the world of learning and development.

I was already in a cracking mood that day as I had received word that a property deal, which I had almost written off as dead and buried two months earlier, had been signed and sealed. The day was going well, but these awards were the stuff of dreams for people in my industry. People like me don't win this kind of stuff, but I had put the effort in, and I was feeling optimistic.

Tom was the host for the evening, so I was already a winner, and I was thinking *he does not know it yet, but I am going to give him a big handshake and even a bear hug.* I am quite a large man and Tom is anything but, so I was not sure how his security would react to me giving him that bear hug. I'd hate to ruin an excellent evening by being dragged off the stage by burly bodyguards.

Our category came around, Best Technology-based Onboarding

Programme, and Tom started announcing the winners with the words, 'And bronze goes to,' but it wasn't us. Next up was the silver, and again, our team was not mentioned. Bronze or silver would have been fine, just for the sake of recognition of the effort put in by my team, but I wanted more. We were there for gold. Tom continued, 'The gold goes to a company and team who have clearly put values at the heart of their design,' and by that stage, I knew it was us. I completed the application, and I presented our ideas to the judging panel, explaining why I believed we deserved the gold award, and I recognised the words that Tom was saying. They were my words!

Seconds later, my team was confirmed as the winner of the gold award, and I jumped up from my chair and let out the biggest, loudest 'Yes' I could ever imagine myself shouting. I am not an overtly emotional kind of guy; maybe it's my military background, maybe it's my difficulty showing vulnerability, or maybe it's both, but I was all out that evening.

Eighteen months earlier, I called out a situation and vowed not only to fix it but to bring about such improvement that I would win external top-of-class recognition for it; the gold award for best technology-based onboarding programme was exactly that. I delivered on my vow, but I did not do it alone, and I was proud to be sitting at the same table as my teammates, especially Charlie, Morten and Rochelle from SolvdTogether, when we were announced as the winners. Charlie and Morten had been with me from the outset of the project, with Rochelle joining the team as soon as we had a plan. It was a first for them as well as me. We were a gold-winning team, and nobody could take that away from us, ever.

WHY TEAMS?

Why not teams? That's where I would start. I have been in teams for much of my working and social life. The Army is built on teamwork unlike many organisations that talk about teamwork yet fail to truly invest internally in their people. As a soldier, you are nothing without your team. The military, where I spent most of my adult working life, delivers blunt force at its most extreme, and that requires boots on the ground, so it is a people business in every way you choose to look at it.

I was an average sportsman, but I enjoyed successes on the sports field as a member of teams that delivered way above the possibilities of the individuals that made those teams up. Humans have understood the power of teamwork since the dawn of civilisation, and countless books have been written about teams, telling us how they work or how to build them and the benefits that they offer. Yet we continue to see organisations failing to capitalise on the potential of not only single teams but the collective impact of multiple teams.

Many organisations comprise many teams carrying out different functions but working symbiotically to achieve shared goals. They achieve more by working harmoniously as a collective. If we start by acknowledging that teams, particularly diverse ones, outperform individuals, we have good reason to want to draw on some of that success for ourselves. It comes down to a simple equation: Collective intelligence (CQ) outguns individual intelligence (IQ): $CQ > IQ$.

As a lifelong member, leader, and benefactor of teams, I have made several key observations.

TEAMS ARE ENERGISED BY SIGNIFICANT PERFORMANCE CHALLENGES AND WANT TO WORK TOGETHER

Members of the team need to feel emotionally connected to the challenge and intrinsically get what the end goal or outcome looks like. That is not to say that the team should not have an opportunity to collectively build what that is, but the challenge must be there from the outset. For the team to achieve those outcomes, it needs the right personal chemistry; that is, each member should want to be a part of the team and enjoy working with the others on the team.

When I was putting my team together for the award-winning programme mentioned above, I wanted people that shared my ambition, shared my desire to deliver experiences that had the customer at the heart of the design, and I wanted to have some fun along the way. I definitely found that when I met initially with Charlie, Morten and Redmond from SolvdTogether. They were a newly formed company, but each one of them came with a lot of experience.

We met for a three-day workshop at my request, partly to accelerate the work but also for me to see if the personalities and team dynamics would work, and they did on every level. Rochelle arrived soon after to bolster our resources and fitted in like a glove. I have been fortunate to have been able to work with them ever since and, indeed, class them all, including the newer members as the team has grown, as friends. CQ at its finest.

Once the emotional connection and buy-in to achieve the goal are established, the team can work on contracting a common set of values or a framework of accountability for each other. This should include a set of behaviours, developed by them, which are specific, discussed frequently, easily understood and bought into by the whole team. With a contract in place, the team can focus on performance, which is the primary objective, while the team remains the means, not the end.

TEAMS ARE HUNGRY FOR COMPETITION

The desire to win fuels motivation, so use this to help drive performance at every level. Set milestones to maintain motivation along the journey. In the military, we referred to this as maintaining momentum, which simply means ensuring that the team continues to move towards the end state or goal. Keep that needle moving in the right direction.

When I was leading the team in the Cambrian Patrol, I shared a common desire with my team to win the gold medal. As we prepared for the patrol, we had to progress through various milestones, such as going further on the hill marches or hitting new team bests for our Friday morning six peaks speed training. Then there was the competition itself. We split the course into several phases and targeted ourselves to complete each section within a set time, so we were always on track to complete the patrol in record time.

TEAMS HAVE SUPERSTARS

Celebrate your superstars, but never let them forget that, as excellent as they are, they are not better than the team—CQ > IQ. On this note, a word of caution is in order. Loyalty cuts both ways, and you can't expect your superstars to sacrifice personal glory for goals they are not invested in. The team has a responsibility to meet its contractual obligations to every member, which includes setting goals that every member wants to achieve. Allow superstars to shine, but make sure their performance is congruent with the performance goals of the team.

The goals of the team should not be antithetical to individual performance. My Cambrian Patrol team included a superstar who was fitter, more experienced, and more highly skilled than every other member of our team, including me, but we were bound by a common competitive goal and a strong contract. During the competition, he had a wobble, and his fitness was tested, but we had the answers in our strong team. Our superstar needed us less shiny stars, but when we won the goal, we all shared the glory equally as agreed in our contract. This is not only a solid example of collective intelligence trumping individual intelligence, but it also highlights how unique situations can challenge us in ways we can't imagine. None of us would have thought that our superstar would come unstuck.

DISCIPLINE, DISCIPLINE, DISCIPLINE

As you can imagine for someone who has dedicated three decades to military service, discipline has been a very close friend to me all my life, even before I signed up for the Army. Any team that is truly seeking the benefits of collective performance must focus on that variable—monitor it, measure it, and strive to improve it. The same can be said for a sportsperson or any individual leader who is seeking to build strong performance standards across their unit or organisation.

The performance outcomes will relate to a set of predetermined requirements based on the analysis of the desired end state, and these should be measurable to enable a process of constant monitoring, accountability, and adjustment.

Discipline is a differentiator in high-performing teams. Those who are disciplined and apply a set of high-performance behaviours will outperform those who do not. No need to boil the ocean on this theory!

Following our initially poor experience of training for the Cambrian Patrol, which was not performance-orientated, we set a new suite of performance-focused goals. Although for three days a week for six weeks, this meant getting up at 0400 hours to be in the mountains at 0600 hours for eight hours of gruelling marching with 40 pounds (eighteen kilograms) on our backs, we did it, and we went into the classroom to study, day in, day out. It was all worth it because results are how we are remembered, and gold is what I call a result.

THE NEED FOR TEAMS

I believe that teams of any size are the basic unit of performance in any organisation, but when I talk about teams, I do not mean bunches of people loosely thrown together with a weak case of identity. Strong teams are bound by a shared sense of purpose and determination to exceed expectations. Most, if not all, situations that need a set of multidisciplinary skills and experiences will be better served by the combined efforts of a team than a set of collective individuals.

Receiving the gold award for best technology-based onboarding programme from Tom Allen meant a lot to me, but let's look at what led to that moment of glory. I had been asked to support a graduate induction programme as a facilitator initially but then purely administratively, which meant stepping back from direct delivery and focusing more on supporting others to facilitate.

The switch left me feeling a bit like a lost sheep, and I didn't like it. I was sent to support a team that was very tightly-knit, incestuous almost, which I understood given their shared history, and it was not a very welcoming atmosphere. Not one to accept a situation I wasn't satisfied with, I reassigned myself the role of feedback machine, and this became my purpose for the next two weeks. I walked the floors, spoke to just about everyone, went to every experience laid on, and soaked it all up.

After two weeks of questioning and observation, the results were in, and I did not like what I had seen. The attendees didn't seem to be impressed with what they were being served up. Over the years, the programme had lost its connection to the target audience, and the only humans who were being considered in the delivery design were the team that I was supposed to be supporting.

I documented my observations in a written report and presented my findings to a very senior business stakeholder, who agreed to meet me for a coffee to discuss the situation. At that meeting, I reiterated my findings, explaining that I felt we were approaching things from the wrong angle and not considering the perspective of the end-users (the attendees) or the best interests of the business. More importantly, I boldly stated that I could do it better and, if she were to allow me to do things my way, we could save the business around three million pounds over three years. She agreed to my proposals on the spot, and Vicky Gallagher-Brown, another senior stakeholder, also lent her support to the new plan. Vicky was with us that night to collect our award.

REMOVE BARRIERS TO SUCCESS

Although I had the green light to proceed with the new approach, I knew I would encounter resistance initially, but I was also fortunate to have the backing of two very powerful stakeholders, and they removed the barriers for me. The main obstructions were people who opposed my way forward, namely those who had been in charge. Although I never laid the blame at their door, it was obvious that under their stewardship, the ship was sinking.

I was careful what I wished for, knowing that once I had been given the responsibility, I would have to deliver, and I was never going to be able to do that on my own. To deliver on such an ambitious project, I would need a team of superstars—enter Charlie and Morten and full access to all the resources that came with SolvdTogether.

Once I found the right people for my team, we set out a contract and established a set of performance outcomes for ourselves, but we also defined the outcomes for our future attendees and the business. I had to build the team virtually as we were spread across the UK, but we set a date for us to meet and spend a few days of practical workshopping to iron out our plan.

WORK AND PLAY AS A TEAM

Of all the things we did over those few days, the only thing that was the work of one person was me expressing my philosophy and outlining my vision of how I saw the experience looking and feeling for those attending our programme. From that moment onwards, we worked on everything together and supported each other when challenged, and there were plenty of challenges to overcome.

Functional teams provide a unique social dynamic that enhances the economic output and the administrative aspects of what they are producing. Once in flow, real teams work hard to overcome common barriers to their success, focused firmly on their shared goal and understanding of what they are working towards, the desired end state. For me, that end state was delivering an award-winning programme that was human-centric.

The final and potentially most enjoyable aspect of working in teams is that they have more fun. Champagne for one does not sound very appealing, whereas sharing the success with teammates in a fancy venue and a great atmosphere... well, that is fun! Never mind the possibility that you might get the chance to bear-hug Tom Allen! In case you're wondering, I spared him the risk of a heart attack and saved myself from the embarrassment of being taken down by security personnel. Tom didn't get the bear hug he so richly deserved!

As long as it is fuelled and sustained by performance, that fun should be there, and success should be celebrated, not just at the end of a project but along the way. Why? It eases the pressures of performance, releases tensions, and may even help to unlock creativity. These benefits will manifest as behavioural changes for the good of the team and ultimately the organisation.

NO PLAN SURVIVES FIRST CONTACT

Members of a highly effective, functional, tightly-knit team are also comfortable with change, even when they need to pivot rapidly. Take the recent Covid-19 situation, for example, and how quickly change was thrust on the world of work, and the performance outputs of teams. The adaptive, end-state-orientated, and highly self-directed teams recognised change requirements and got on with the necessary shift quickly, resetting the model without upsetting the rhythm. This happened to my team, and we had to conjure up an alternative delivery model for the plan we had been working on.

When Covid-19 impacted our delivery plans, we adapted as expected; in fact, we did what was not expected by delivering something ground-breaking that has changed the standards across the entire firm. How did we do this? Well, the delivery model was not the end state, the quality of the programme was the end state, and that is what we were focused on. The plan changed, not the end state or desired outcome. No plan survives first contact is a military phrase that simply means that no matter how much you plan, it will often have to change, so be ready to adjust always.

We will consider in depth the role of the leader within teams in a later chapter, but it's worth acknowledging here that teams need leadership, and the question to consider is style—a command and control or connect and coach approach. The answer will, of course, depend on the nature of the team and the organisation, but leadership style should be part of the initial consideration when building the team resources and then how those resources build their contracting agreement internally and externally within the organisation. An intelligently designed team comprising quality talent will be far better equipped to self-manage, and the leadership-power distance will be much smaller; therefore, a coaching-orientated approach is likely to be more successful.

WHAT DO THE SUCCESS FACTORS LOOK LIKE?

SET DIRECTION

They know their purpose, why they exist, and what they need to accomplish. In the example above, my team had a clear mandate: We would design and deliver an industry-leading, award-winning onboarding programme. It was simple and effective, and it meant that all our activity was cross-checked against it.

NO *I* IN TEAM

The tasks that need to be done should require team members to work together. If team members do not work together, they risk being in a team by name only and not working collectively, failing to benefit from the collective intelligence available.

REWARD TEAM EXCELLENCE

Celebrate the wins, however small—a milestone, a new round of funding or organisational support. The rewards and celebrations are to be shared across the team. When celebrating an individual for performance, it should be a reward for performance in supporting the team.

SUPPORT THE RESOURCE DEMANDS

If the team needs something, make it available if possible. A lack of resources can mean a lack of progress and subsequently impact performance.

ADOPT A MISSION COMMAND PHILOSOPHY

> *I found that delegation of responsibility to the lowest possible level produces results out of all proportion to the risk involved in letting junior people have a measure of independence and authority.*
>
> General Sir John Harding, Chief of the Imperial General Staff

This is a military philosophy but an equally relevant approach for any team. It is simply the distribution or delegation of authority by the organisation or its leader to the lowest possible level. This harnesses trust in the team to get the job done while remaining firmly focused on the mission or the end state.

HARNESS THE POWER OF DIVERSITY AND EQUALITY, AND BE INCLUSIVE

The more diverse the team is, the greater the pool of skills available. Remember diversity of thought, which is often overlooked, when considering the diversity markers of a new team.

RESPECT AND TRUST

Linked to the principles of diversity, equality, and inclusion is the importance of mutual respect for individuals within the team. Respect leads to the development of trust, which is vitally important to the organisation investing in the team.

PERFORM LIKE STARS IN A BLOCKBUSTER MOVIE

Some of the teams I have been privileged to be a part of have delivered results that no one on the outside looking in could have imagined. I love working in teams and having taken numerous psychometric tests, I score highly as a raging ideas person with strong traits for building teams. Unsurprisingly, I have come to not just accept but relish the opportunity to collaborate with others as I have learnt to love the skin I occupy.

To deliver the skills to support my ideas and bring them to fruition, I have needed the help of strong, effective teams, and I have loved sharing the successes along the way. I have learnt a lot from others that I wouldn't have without the opportunity to work in teams. I believe that everyone has something to contribute to collective intelligence, and I hope that everyone gets a chance to be in a team, especially one that succeeds on every level.

The insights and recommendations I have outlined in this chapter are based on my training and experience within teams. While not exhaustive, they can help leaders to build great teams that achieve their full potential and perform like stars in a blockbuster movie.

The next chapter explores moments that matter or moments of truth. When we are faced with unexpected dilemmas and quandaries, when should we and how should we respond?

Moments
That Matter

You could go to any busy high street and ask one hundred people to tell you what business they are in, and you'd get one hundred different answers, even from people in the same industry. But however different we may all be, we have at least two things in common.

Firstly, we are all part of the human race. Some are running the race for themselves, and some are running it for others, but they all are in the race. The second thing is that we all experience moments that matter, really matter. We need to recognise these moments for what they are and not miss them in the blur of life and everyday activity. Most, if not all of those moments, relate to how we affect those around us.

MOMENTS MATTER

I have experienced many moments that matter. Some I have recognised and done something about, others I have missed and regretted, and there are many missed moments that I still regret and am dealing with today. One of these occurred during my time in Sierra Leone.

We were under strict orders not to help beggars or give charitably—*harsh*, I hear you say, and I agree now at least, but there was a strong philosophical reason for this directive. We were there to help them help themselves. As the well-known saying goes, we could hand a fish to a hungry man only to find that he'd be back the next day looking for another fish. It's better to give him a fishing rod and teach him how to fish, so he can feed his family forever.

It was a hot afternoon, and I was driving past an orphanage in my Land Rover when I heard a rapping on the door. A child was running alongside the vehicle and when I looked down at him, I noticed that he had lost both his hands. This was no ordinary orphanage; it was for children who had lost limbs in the war.

The civil war was brutal in every way, and one of the cruellest aspects of the conflict was the number of children who were enlisted to fight. Children aged between eight and fourteen were recruited on all sides. They were easy to persuade because there was only one thing worse than being in a war zone with an AK47 and having to kill or be killed, and that was being in a war zone without an AK47, no army to protect them, and no food to eat.

If a child was too young to fight, their hands were cut off at the wrist to ensure they couldn't be taken to fight for another faction later. I don't know about you, but I consider a situation where children have a choice between starving to death, being shot or maimed, or having to fight in a war as being as close to hell on earth as it gets.

All that child wanted was a little help. I could have and arguably should have helped, but I didn't even stop the vehicle. I complied with my orders, not my heart. To this day and every day, I can see that little boy, who was probably about the same age as my youngest son, knocking on the side of my Land Rover with a stump where his hand should have been. Even now, I feel myself welling up with a combination of sadness that another human could do this to such an innocent little boy and the fact that I failed to help him.

That moment mattered to me on so many levels. It mattered to me then, and it has mattered ever since, so much so that I made a couple of solemn vows. One, I vowed to do my best to deliver a long-standing solution to the security situation that the collapse of Sierra Leone had brought about and prevent further terrible suffering for the people living there. Two, I vowed to never walk past another situation like that again, orders or no orders. I am a soldier through and through, and a good one, but the standard that we walk past is the standard that we accept, and I did not accept this ever again. That's my line, so to hell with any future orders to the contrary.

A lot has happened since then, and I will share some of that later. For now, I'm asking you to reflect on any occasions or moments that mattered where you walked past without doing what you could have done. Let's not allow that to happen again.

Over the next few pages, I will share some of the moments or opportunities that I have encountered that I have managed to make matter. My moments that matter may help you to spot similar opportunities when they knock at your door.

WALKING IN THEIR SHOES

Walking in their shoes is not simply about trying on someone else's size tens and thinking *nah, not for me, tried them but they don't fit*. It is about empathy, not sympathy—two very different things. Sympathy is feeling sorry for someone and perhaps offering advice or solutions disguised as concern. Empathy, on the other hand, is feeling the situation as though you were them. The good news is that we can learn the difference, and more importantly, we can learn the skills needed to be empathetic. Walking in their shoes can also help us when we are confronted with a difficult situation. This reminds me of an incident that took place while I was serving in Northern Ireland.

I heard my callsign over the radio from HQ (a callsign, such as Mike Tango 0A, is an identifier, often used in radio communcation. My orders were to move to a street location and escort a police officer to an address to deliver a court summons. This sounds innocuous, but we were about to go into a very difficult area where we were definitely not welcome.

We picked up the police officer and headed to our destination. All was quiet to start with, and the officer managed to deliver the summons, but within seconds, a minute at most, a crowd had gathered, and they were on us very quickly. My mind was racing. *How the fuck do we get out of here now?* There were only twelve of us and one police officer, but we were facing a mob of dozens. I jumped straight to full aggressive action and instructed the drivers to position the vehicles in a charge configuration. Well, as you can imagine, this sent the crowd nuts. Bricks and missiles were soon raining in on us.

We were wearing riot gear, so I got out of my armoured truck and gave orders to follow my vehicle down the street, push the crowd back, and get out of there sharp. Our job was done, and I didn't need to be embroiled in a riot. I felt secure with my protective gear on, so I marshalled each surge of about ten metres. We were making steady progress towards the exit point at the bottom of the street.

Bang! A searing pain exploded from my ankle as though I had been stabbed with a red-hot poker. The sensation was so intense, it radiated through my entire being, almost blinding me from everything else. A rock had smashed into one of the few areas not protected by my body armour, striking the bone and lighting up the nerve endings that were highly concentrated on the surface of the skin. Despite the feeling of fire in my lower left leg, I could not risk showing any weakness. With what felt like everything I had, I jumped into the vehicle, and we were away.

On reflection, what did I do? I escalated the situation to the highest level instantly and angered the crowd, and, as you'd expect, they reacted in the same way. Every action has an equal and opposite reaction, I recall from my early physics classes. I don't think Newton had civil unrest in mind when he discovered his third law of motion, but I saw it in action that day in Northern Ireland.

If I had been walking in their shoes, I would have seen that we looked and behaved aggressively and so that's how we were perceived, and that's why we were met with aggression. Instead of escalating the situation, I should have recognised that they perceived us as a threat and taken action to assure them that we weren't a threat and would be leaving as soon as the police officer had completed their task.

I'm not naive enough to suggest that things may not have still escalated. We were not wanted, and I'm confident they were just as unhappy with someone being served a warrant as by our presence, but we didn't have to be the ones to turn the heat up. I misjudged the situation, didn't see it from their perspective or take time to think about how our presence may have made them feel, and on top of all that, my approach lacked balance. One very sore ankle later and some time to reflect have taught me a very important lesson. Walk in their shoes!

BE PRESENT

Every day, we encounter moments that need or deserve our full attention—physically, emotionally, and intellectually. This may mean interrupting something we are doing or giving time when it is precious. When these moments arise, it is important to recognise and prioritise them and show up with our whole selves.

Stephen Covey, in his well-known book *The 7 Habits of Highly Effective People*, said, 'Most people do not listen with the intent to understand; they listen with the intent to reply.' I am sure we have all fallen short of what is needed to be truly present, and I have certainly been guilty of this.

We need to pick up on the signs that tell us we are not present. Look out for mobile phone distractions, thinking about our own issues and next moves, lack of preparation for the situation we are going into, and, on a very basic level, our attitude towards the situation.

I have a friend who is so tied to his mobile phone that having a conversation with him is nearly impossible without being interrupted by a vibration or beep from his phone to notify him of a message. Even in silent mode, the screen lighting up with some image will rob his attention. *So what*, you may be thinking; *that's life as we know it, Steve!* Okay, but it doesn't have to be that way. Pay attention, turn off notifications or even turn the device over, prepare for the situation, and get your head in the game. You could perhaps even consider walking in the shoes of the people you are with, and ask yourself how you would feel if they weren't mentally present; not great, I'm guessing!

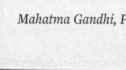

Be the change that you wish to see in the world.

Mahatma Gandhi, Political and Civil Rights Leader,
Social and Spiritual Activist

When we change our behaviour, we change the example we are setting. As Gandhi put it so perfectly, be the change that you wish to see in the world. For example, we could start a meeting with, 'Great to see everyone. We have a jam-packed agenda to get through, and I really want to hear from everyone, so let's close the laptops, turn off the mobiles, or at least turn them over, and give each other the time and attention we need for this meeting.'

When I am at home with my family in the evening, I set a time to put the mobile away in a cupboard. Sometimes I have to work late, and I let my loved ones know in advance and ask for their understanding. Likewise, however, and more importantly, I agree that once I have stopped working, I will be fully present for whatever may follow, whether that's playtime with my boys or time to chat and watch some television with my wife.

PLAY TO YOUR AUDIENCE

There's nothing more welcoming than being in an environment that feels like it's been specially prepared for us; 'where everybody knows your name', as Gary Portnoy and Judy Hart sang in the well-known theme tune to the classic American sitcom *Cheers*. It's about belonging and feeling special. To create that kind of atmosphere, we need a high degree of situational awareness.

In my early days of military training, I was introduced to the Estimate Process, a toolkit used in military planning, and it has served me well in my professional and personal lives ever since. On many occasions, this process has prompted me to check for changes in the situation and adjust my plan or approach accordingly.

A key component of the broader Estimate Process is the Seven Questions Estimate. This is a military process, and there is a huge pile of subheadings and additional details for soldiers to consider. For this book, I am only interested in the first of these questions, which, in simple terms, is about considering the situation and how it affects us.

In one of my military roles, as an infantry tactics instructor at Infantry School Headquarters, I was training newly commissioned officers from Sandhurst. My job, which I found very rewarding, was to help them gain the skills needed to command a platoon of soldiers and hopefully avoid the sort of mistakes, which, in the infantry world, can cause serious injury and death.

On one occasion, I was teaching the Law of Subtension, which is used to adjust mortar fire on the battlefield. Mortars are portable weapons that are used to launch explosive shells at targets from a distance. Shells are loaded into a tube or barrel, which is mounted on a base plate that is placed on the ground and stabilised with a bipod or tripod. The angle of the barrel is adjusted to change the range of the weapon.

The Law of Subtension is not rocket science, projectile science perhaps, but one of my students was just not getting it. He was the only one struggling to grasp the concept, but it was my responsibility to get everyone over the finish line. I remember talking about it to my then-girlfriend, now wife, Gillian, who was and still is a dedicated early years teacher. She told me to prepare at least two ways of teaching the method and to imagine how a child would think about it. What a great piece of insight! I took her advice, and it has served me well for a quarter of a century.

Thinking like a child led me to a foolproof way of explaining the Law of Subtension. The whiteboard was put to one side and replaced with a bin and some screwed-up pieces of paper. We took turns throwing the paper balls at the bin and when we missed, we looked at how to correct our action to get it right. Rather than blaming the student, I applied situational awareness and concluded that neither of us was the problem. A very simple adjustment to the delivery of the training took away the pressure, made an abstract idea more tangible and fun to learn, and delivered excellent results.

REVERSE THE LENS

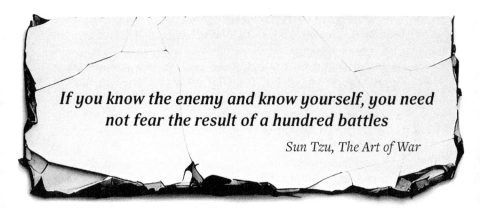

If you know the enemy and know yourself, you need not fear the result of a hundred battles

Sun Tzu, *The Art of War*

The Art of War, the comprehensive guide to planning and executing military campaigns written by the Chinese military strategist and philosopher Sun Tzu, was compulsory reading while I was studying at Sandhurst. Given that it is estimated to have been drafted at least two-and-a-half millennia ago, very few military strategy books have stood the test of time like Sun Tzu's.

When considering Sun Tzu's quote about knowing the enemy and knowing ourselves, my training officers asked us to look at our plans from the enemy's perspective or to imagine them looking at us through their weapons scopes. What does this mean for our day-to-day, and why should we pay attention to it?

On a personal level, imagining the other person's perspective helps us to build meaningful relationships, strengthens our emotional intelligence, and possibly most importantly, improves our understanding of empathy, which I believe is the most essential skill in the EQ spectrum. From a business perspective, there are several hats or lenses that we can consider:

- Stakeholders—these include our competitors, customers, others in the leadership hierarchy, and our team. This is a valuable exercise for everyone, not just leaders.
- The Big Picture—zoom out and look at the wider implications of the situation. Look for the specified tasks that must be done

and consider any implied tasks that we may turn into opportunities. The implied tasks show us how we can improve by fixing issues or upgrading systems. For example, when a kiosk vendor sells coffee to take away, providing a container is an implied task. This provides the vendor with the opportunity to offer a reusable cup!

- The Alternative—turn your thoughts, plans or actions and consequences on their head, and consider the opposite perspective.
- Back to the Future—not that we need to get as complex as the movie franchise, but consider what the consequences of your actions or plans might be in the future. How might your actions be considered on reflection?
- Tales of the Unexpected—you have several courses of action available to you, so which one do you choose? Don't forget that other options still exist whether you can see them or not. If a course of action is not right, then it is not right, but extend your thinking. You don't have to go with the obvious or expected one.

You have no choice but to consider at least one of the lenses mentioned above if you are in the business of serving clients or customers. If you are a parent, friend, sibling, son, or daughter, you will definitely benefit from looking through more than one lens (the more, the merrier), even if that means nothing more than being better informed.

COLLABORATE FOR BETTER RESULTS

Answer this question for yourself; there are no prizes: How many times have you been in a room with other people or members of your team and found that you are more intelligent than all of them put together? I know the answer for myself, and it is a very big 'NEVER'. The concept of collective intelligence means, in its most basic form, using the people around you to gain the best results. When we do this with aplomb, we not only share the work; we share the outcomes, the pressures, the benefits and more often than not, the optimum results. What's not to like? To achieve this, we do, of course, need to be adept at managing the room and the personalities in it. This is culture over couture.

In my personal life and career, I have always wanted to, and have been able to build successful teams. Maybe it is self-awareness of my technical limitations that makes me do this, but I prefer to think it is that I know the value of collective intelligence. I want to arrive at the best solution for the problems that I face, whether that means leveraging the collective intelligence of the team, hiring people who bring a different perspective or contracting specialists to turn creative thinking into a reality.

I have worked with many different types of people and companies, but they have all brought insights that have helped to deliver game-changing results. This kind of collaboration has led to nationally recognised awards for the work we have done, together! I could write a book on this topic alone as it has touched so much of my life, but, for now, I will share the words of Tenzin Gyatso, the fourteenth Dalai Lama: 'We human beings are social beings. We come into the world as the result of others' actions. We survive here in dependence on others. Whether we like it or not, there is hardly a moment in our lives when we do not benefit from others' activities. For this reason, it is hardly surprising that most of our happiness arises in the context of our relationships with others.'

SERVICE BEFORE SELF

This means putting others first, and it can be applied to business, clients, family, or friends, but to sacrifice self-interest for the good of others is quite a challenge and one that is embedded in culture, not doctrine or policy. I am going to say more about this in a later chapter, so, for now, trust me when I say that placing self-interest to one side and asking what the best outcome would be for them will be a great start!

TAKE POSSESSION—OWN THE PROBLEM,
OWN THE SOLUTION

We are all leaders, even at the lowest level of leading ourselves! This means taking ownership of our actions and our results, the disappointing as well as the impressive ones, and it is most difficult when the results are poor. Scary as it might sound, taking ownership of the issue and accepting responsibility for the solution is often seen as evidence of confidence, capability, and commitment, otherwise known as The Three Cs of ownership. On the flip side, we must be aware that an unwillingness or resistance to owning an issue will be due to another troublesome trio of mental barriers—fear, avoidance, and denial.

THE THREE CS—
CONFIDENCE, CAPABILITY, AND COMMITMENT

Looked at more closely, we can see that these three attributes are the antidote to the energy-sapping effects of fear, avoidance, and denial. As we grow in confidence, our fear wains. Strengthening our capability boosts our confidence, which in turn makes us less likely to avoid challenges. Making a solid commitment to ourselves and others ties us into a contract that makes it much harder to deny our responsibilities. The three Cs are the antithesis of fear, avoidance, and denial.

ALWAYS IMPROVING

I pride myself on being a lifelong learner. Writing this book is a prime example of that, and it has been a steep learning curve. I breezed through school, and by the time I left, much of my potential was left unfulfilled. My early work experience was one of continuous growth, however, as I strove for improvement every day, every week, every month, and every year. That process of steady gains continued into my military career and took me from strength to strength and promotion after promotion. My corporate career has challenged and enriched me in other ways, helping me to grow into the person I am today.

That all sounds like a bed of roses, but it wasn't. There were plenty of challenges, and had I not been so determined, competitive, and laser-focused (on not ending up back where I started as a kid), things may have turned out differently. History is written by the victors, and so many of the stories I am sharing in this book relate to times when I overcame the odds, navigated tough situations, or bounced back from the brink of disaster. Have there been regrets? Yes. Missed opportunities? Definitely, but I can recognise them, and I am not afraid to look myself in the eye and ask what I learnt and how I can do things better next time because I know there will be a next time, and I will be prepared for it.

The thing that connects the infinite number of moments that we all have in our lives is the opportunity for growth. Every decision counts, and if we want those choices to be good ones that benefit us, we need to adopt and nurture a growth mindset. We are constantly surrounded by opportunities, even when things appear to be threats and challenges on the surface.

I was in my forties when I enrolled for a master's degree in Business Administration (MBA) at Queens University Belfast. Studying for an MBA was never about gaining a piece of paper. I didn't need the qualification, but I needed to prove to myself that I was capable of the academic rigour that gaining such a prestigious qualification from a Russell Group university demands.

One year later, I did gain that MBA, but it was a weekly struggle to keep up with the submissions. Academic study has taught me that the wider our perspectives are, the more well-rounded we are. My professor, Mark Palmer, who led our programme, announced on the first day that this course would be transformational! The uneducated sceptic in me scoffed at the idea. *Really? I have been on a battlefield and run my own business, and these are transformational, but some lectures and a few words here and there... transformative?* Yes. Really!

There have been three major transformational learning incidents in my life, but the most significant of these was my time spent gaining an MBA. It broadened and deepened my spectrum of thinking, and I have Mark to thank for that. He gave me a place on that course when others would not have as I didn't have an undergraduate degree. I managed to fast-track my way to an MBA from GCSEs with a twenty-seven-year gap in between!

Moments matter. How will you make them matter more in your world starting now?

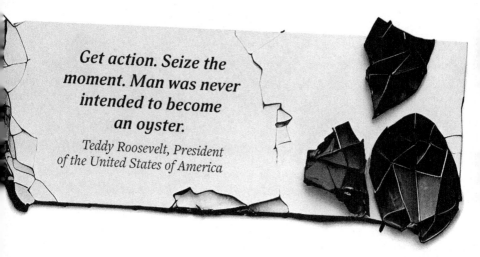

Get action. Seize the moment. Man was never intended to become an oyster.

Teddy Roosevelt, President of the United States of America

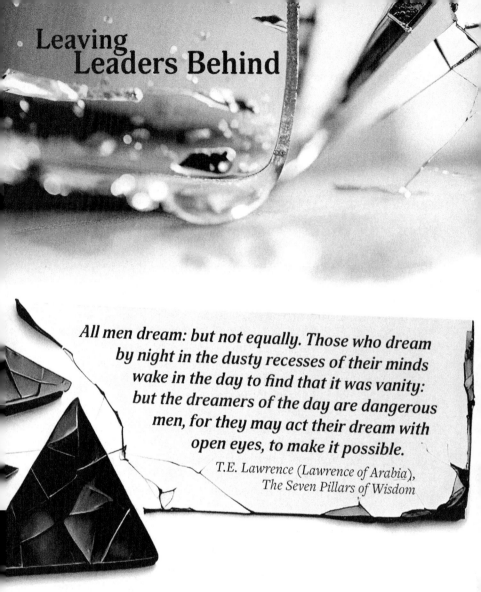

Leaving
Leaders Behind

All men dream: but not equally. Those who dream by night in the dusty recesses of their minds wake in the day to find that it was vanity: but the dreamers of the day are dangerous men, for they may act their dream with open eyes, to make it possible.

T.E. Lawrence (Lawrence of Arabia),
The Seven Pillars of Wisdom

Leaders are action-orientated, but the actions they take don't always inspire the people they are supposedly leading to behave in the way they would like them to. We are all leaders, some more reluctant than others. At the most fundamental level, leadership starts with the self, and we must be able to take charge of ourselves before we can lead others effectively.

In this chapter, we are going to take a practical look at leadership, drawing on real-life situations that I have directly observed. As the military is often referenced in discussions about leadership, I will share my thoughts based primarily on my experiences in the Army. That said, I appreciate that there have been incidents in military history that have not been such great examples of leadership, so I will share warts-and-all accounts and analyses wherever possible in the interest of completeness and objectivity.

We will then begin to explore some of the critical elements in my own evolving model of personal leadership, resilience and capability.

LEADERSHIP VERSUS MANAGEMENT

There is so much research available that I don't need to wade into the many arguments that persist within the field of leadership, which, in my opinion, have yet to be definitively resolved. One of these debates revolves around the concept of leadership versus management and the virtues of each. During my time in service, which includes nine and a half years of accumulated active military service around the world (i.e., time spent in operational deployments as opposed to time in barracks), I have seen great managers become great leaders and talented managers who possessed leadership potential but did not wish to take on leadership roles.

On the flip side, I have seen excellent leaders who exhibited superb management skills. Based on my experiences, I have only one thing to offer to the management-versus-leadership discussion: simply that the distinction between these two roles is primarily a matter of opportunity. In other words, an effective manager who has not had the opportunity to lead will only ever be a great manager. You get the point, right?

LEADERSHIP CREDENTIALS

When I am delivering leadership modules in programmes that I run, I often open the sessions with a very simple question: Why would anyone follow you? I then let the room ponder on it for two minutes before asking the first volunteer to stand and share their answer with the room. This should be easy, right? After all, they are leaders, so their Why should be easily articulated and announced in a confident, charismatic manner. Or so you would think. Actually, the opposite is more often the case, and my request for a volunteer is sometimes met with silence, fear, and prayers for an invisibility cloak in the hope that I will not come and stand beside them for the answer.

I am, of course, only playing with them, but there is a good reason why they should be able to answer that question. Leaders need followers to legitimately maintain the title or status of leader. Much as leadership starts with self, I can't call myself an effective leader simply for exercising the self-discipline to rise at five every morning and stick to a carefully planned routine of yoga, Callanetics, and an ice bath! That's not my regimen, in case you're wondering. Today's institutes are much less hierarchical, and, therefore, leaders cannot rely solely on rank or position, not in isolation at least. They need to know what it is that will engage their people and rouse commitment and loyalty to their company, cause, or purpose.

A VERY BRIEF HISTORY OF THINKING AROUND LEADERSHIP

Society has always been fascinated by leadership and hungry for knowledge on the subject. From Julius Caesar (100-44 BCE) to Cleopatra VII (69-30 BCE), Charlemagne (768-814 CE) to Queen Elizabeth I (1533-1603 CE), Emperor Qin Shi Huang (259-210 BCE) of China, Genghis Khan (1162-1227 CE) of Mongolia, Mahatma Gandhi (1869-1948 CE) of India, Franklin D. Roosevelt (1882-1945 CE) of the United States of America, Nelson Mandela (1918-2013 CE) of South Africa, and, of course, Great Britain's very own Winston Churchill (1874-1965 CE), the world has never been short of great leaders!

Sun Tzu's *The Art of War*, which he wrote at some point between the sixth and fifth centuries before the common era (BCE), provides all the evidence you need that human beings appreciate and want to improve as leaders. Like any subject of learning, thinking around leadership has evolved and that will continue as we discover more about human psychology and behaviour.

In the 1920s, we start to see some serious interest in deepening the research around leadership: moving from trait theory, which attempted to identify common traits and characteristics of so-called effective leaders. Trait theory gave way to style theory (authoritarian, democratic, and laissez-faire), and contemporary thinking is dominated by contingency theory, which starts from the position that leadership is dependent on the situation, not unlike what I said about leadership arising from the opportunity to rise to the occasion. According to contingency theory, how someone leads will depend on a wide range of factors including the type of challenge they face and the people they wish to lead.

After my regular military service and a bit of a gap, I joined the Reserve Army. Everything was new to me, the mix of regular Army staff with part-time soldiers and officers. It was something that I had never really sought to understand, the dynamic of this environment, let alone how it all worked.

My initial experience was a bit allergic if I am being completely open, and I nearly left after one training weekend. It all seemed a bit ad-hoc; no planning, professionally a bit loose, certainly with the officer level I was working with, and to put it bluntly, very self-serving with no sign of putting the soldiers first. I struggled with this. As a regular officer, you are drilled on service before self, and that means the soldiers' needs are met first. In barracks, that means training them, looking after their career development, and being an example for them to follow as they grow. The leadership was not only bad; it was toxic. I have had anger issues for much of my life, perhaps because that's how I am hardwired or because it took time to calm down after a tricky start, and I am big enough to admit this, but I believe the anger I felt at how these soldiers were being treated was fully justified.

Military leadership training is comprehensive, and the expectations and behaviours of its leaders are high, so there is no excuse for what I witnessed on joining my new Army Reserve unit. Leadership is the lifeblood of any military unit, organisation, or body. It is the spirit that develops its people, builds teams and relationships, and importantly gets results on behalf of those teams and organisations. While difficult to define, leadership in the eyes of the Army is a combination of character, knowledge and actions that inspires others to succeed. I raised a few of my concerns, and very quickly my commanding officer had me appointed to command the company of men and women I had joined, with the explicit task of 'Go fix it, then, Steve!' So, where do you start on something like this? Well, how do you eat an elephant? One bite at a time!

COURAGE

The chaos that surrounds failing organisations is often an indicator that something is not right, and the root cause is often, but not always, its leadership. We're back to that age-old issue: If we want to change the fruit, we need to change the root. Change of this nature, whether it be the leadership style or the leader that needs to be transformed, requires courage. In the situation that I was facing, both needed changing, and it would take bold and courageous actions from me and others within the organisation if we were to effect a positive turnaround.

I remember sitting with my in-place leadership team and describing what I had observed within the organisation and what my ambitions were. For some, it was hard to hear as they were part of the problem; if they could open their ears and minds and embrace the change, they could be part of the solution. For others, it was daunting but exciting, and I could see their enthusiasm for the fix.

This was not new territory for me, having had to address a similar environmental issue in Sierra Leone where neither the culture nor climate aligned with a values-driven ethos. Looking every one of them in the eyes, I promised to invest everything I had in the journey and asked the same of them with one unemotional caveat: If any individual proved not to have the skills or the energy to do what was required, I would not hesitate to remove them from the team, not in a destructive manner but for the greater good of the soldiers who looked to us as their leaders.

Courage is an essential characteristic for any leader, and they need plenty of it, morally and physically. The values and standards of a leader should be reflected in everything they do and in the organisations they lead.

The physical courage of a leader is essential to overcome or prevail when faced with stressful situations and there will be many. For those in the military, overcoming personal fears means facing potentially life-threatening situations. In the corporate world, the very act of taking on the mantle of leadership is challenging and frightening. The fear is real in both cases, even though the threats are different, and the effects of that fear on the body and mind are the same. Physical courage is infectious, though, and leaders who set an example by displaying it influence those observing it by fortifying their tolerance for adversity.

Moral courage is arguably even more important and the one most likely to be tested. Simply put, moral courage is the willingness to do the right thing and make the difficult decisions, always! If we consider moral courage as the currency of respect, then every time we display it, we are investing in our personal bank of respect, which attracts other investors, and that is when good behaviours become instinctive.

It is not good enough to do the right thing most of the time. Moral courage must be maintained with an unshakeable consistency. As leaders, we must do the right thing all the time, even when we think no one is watching. We have all fallen short at one time or another, but the big question is this: If you are reading this as a leader or while considering future leadership roles and opportunities for you and your organisation, do you have the courage to up your game?

I left a full complement of very capable leaders behind when I left my squadron, having told them at the outset that they would know when my time was up when they no longer needed me to lead the organisation. Do you have the character to be a values-driven leader who oozes physical and moral courage? If you are still reading and considering what your answer would be, then I think you do!

VULNERABILITY AND AUTHENTICITY

'Vulnerability is weakness! Discuss.'

If that was the exam question, how would you go about answering it; would you look to the empirical evidence, would you look internally at your own definition, or would you open yourself up to go and get qualitative evidence from the people in your life?

The chances are that you will conclude that vulnerability is weakness and arrive at a set of insights on how you might address the said weakness. Here is an alternative viewpoint. Our starting point should be that there is little to no evidence that supports the view that vulnerability is weakness. It is not a question of success or failure; it is having the courage to show up in situations that have no defined outcomes or controls. It is perfectly natural to feel vulnerable in such situations as, quite literally, anything can happen.

As an Army officer, I had plenty of vulnerable moments, despite being well-trained and drilled in how I might deal with certain situations of the aggressive kind or, as was sometimes the case, the more emotional experiences of other people's vulnerabilities on open display. Being vulnerable or experiencing situations that increase our vulnerability is not easy; we can feel uncertain, threatened, anxious, and even downright frightened for our safety. That is when we rely on our courage, both moral and physical.

I was vulnerable when I took on the responsibility of turning my reserve squadron around. I needed those reserves to show up for me. Otherwise, I would fall flat on my face. I offered up what I knew and what I would give and asked for support from those who could plug the gaps that I came with. It was also important for them to trust me just as I would be putting my trust in their leadership team, and I asked them for that trust along with forgiveness for the mistakes that I would make along the way, acknowledging that I was a work in progress.

I also asked for an open and continuous feedback loop. Do not dismiss feedback as an opportunity to criticise unwanted or poor behaviours. It is a tool for improvement. When marshalled correctly, it is a mechanism to right the wayward trajectory of your course of action. Feedback should be viewed as a privilege and should be offered promptly, delivered with a warm heart, motivated by a willingness to do things better, and never to deliberately do harm. To love, or to have passion or ambitions is to be vulnerable, so you'd better be ready to embrace it if you want to chase any of these! Vulnerability is real and should be embraced as a strength in leadership. It is anything but a weakness, but it is not something you can turn off anyway. You will not succeed on your own—that's not how we are wired—but you can optimise team cohesion by embracing vulnerability together and using it as a catalyst for building trust, and we need trust as leaders and team members.

RELATIONSHIP-BUILDING

Leaders need followers and therefore need to build relationships. Building self-awareness as a leader matters and helps with the process of relationship-building. Learning from the experiences we encounter on our life journeys is a messy process, but it's essential for understanding our personal brand, who we are, and how we lead. Do this well, and we are on the way to being truly empathetic leaders.

The establishment of a leader's legitimacy will be based on their competence and trustworthiness, as we discussed earlier. No competency, no trust. No trust, no followers. These are the fundamental building blocks for leader-follower relationships. Once competency and trust have been established, the relationship needs to be cultivated. The leader needs to be an exemplary supervisor who motivates from a performance perspective while allowing the follower to perform with freedom.

This comes back to the concept of mission command that we looked at in depth in the chapter concerning setting clear expectations. We can see how adopting a mission command approach depends on solid relationships built on trust and competence but also helps to strengthen relationships and build that trust. We see this increasingly now in government when local authorities are given the power to execute their plans autonomously within central policy and or budget.

An empathetic leader will also need to accurately judge the needs of the team, their capacity, and their capabilities.

Finally, and only once all the above has been achieved, the leader has a clear responsibility to ensure that the relationships are equitable, fair, and inclusive.

If a leader can achieve these things, they can begin the process of development of capability, capacity, and loyalty across the follower landscape. Leaders must provide ongoing guidance but only at the level required—too much guidance risks eroding trust; too little leaves the follower vulnerable to error. They must be engaged and promote the feedback loops because feedback provides the opportunity to engage directly with individuals and the team to ensure that they are building a positive self-evaluating, result-orientated ethos. Leaders must also deploy the resources available to them intelligently and efficiently. Use your best to help them to do their best! If you can do this, you, your followers, and ultimately the organisation will reap the benefits of the strong relationships that deliver the sort of results we saw in the chapter, Building Blockbuster Teams, where those collective efforts far outweigh the possibilities of the individual.

As I write, it is two years since I left my squadron, and I am still in contact with my key leadership teams and often meet up with them for a beer and a catch-up. I loved them for what we achieved together, and it makes me laugh that even now they still call me *Boss*, a term of endearment for those officers lucky enough to have crafted enough trust of their followers. I am truly honoured to have served for and with them.

Knowing what you know now, what importance do you put on building relationships? Think, reflect on what you have just read, and ask yourself whether you are doing enough.

INTELLIGENCE IN LEADERSHIP

Leadership research has never really focused on a specific skill or personality trait that leaders must have to be successful; however, intelligence is widely acknowledged to be a key element, and, in recent years, it has been seen as more of a process, with several considerations or cognitive resources that can be learnt and deployed to maximise the impact of the role of leader. In simple terms, being smart is not just about what you know; it's about using your brain in different ways to be the best leader you can be, and many aspects of leadership are learnable. For this, I am truly glad as I left school at sixteen with a few paltry GCSEs (General Certificates of Secondary Education). I fully appreciate they do not tell the whole story regarding my intelligence, but they do reflect the attitude I held towards the usefulness of formal education at that time.

I have navigated my life and career by using a seemingly invisible framework. At least, it was invisible to me as I never took any cognitive steps towards utilising my intellect. I felt my way through, almost instinctively, driven by goals. Sure, I discovered a kind of predictive machine even before I was a man, setting the goal, establishing what I needed to do to get there, and getting on with it, but I was ashamed of my low level of academic achievement.

My failure to do better at school has been a bit of a ball and chain for me throughout my personal and professional life. Over that time, I have often felt that I was not good enough. I was good enough, and that makes it even more infuriating on a personal level, as I was allowed to decide to leave school at sixteen instead of being effectively encouraged to stick with it. Having fallen way short of my academic potential, it took twenty-six years for me to bury that demon. In 2014, I gained an MBA at Queens University Belfast, and the stalker that was academic mediocracy was buried for good.

Letting go of the limitations of my self-defined academic inadequacy has allowed me to reflect with real focus. As a result, my *invisible* framework of leadership in life and business has been appearing, element by element, concept by concept, process by process. At this point I invite you to explore your leadership experience and capability through the following perspectives.

At this point I share this with you simply to help you start noticing and making sense of the underlying dynamics of the challenges and brilliant results you've witnessed in your own journey. When you reflect upon your own experience, the model will begin to reveal itself more clearly, just as it has within me.

THE FOUNDATIONS OF PERSONAL LEADERSHIP

Personal leadership, its relationship with organisational demands, structures and processes, and its interplay with teams has been evolving over many years. My own experience, research, reading, and ruminations have intrinsically evolved my approach to leadership.

Whilst the initial concepts we've explored thus far—cognitive intelligence, emotional intelligence and collective intelligence—are widely recognised, when it comes to moving beyond the standard approach, we need to set our sights further and deeper.

When dealing with challenging areas we are tempted to oversimplify things which creates distorted results and problems down the line. Or we tend to experience the paralysis of overwhelm when we recognise the true complexity that exists.

You operate in a complex world of interrelated systems and human beings who are incredibly varied and dynamic—as a leader you need a way to develop your own leadership capability for the sake of the organisation's goals, the flourishing of the people involved, and your own, long-term satisfaction and well-being.

In terms of serving your team, growing the market impact of

your organisation and being a more assured leader, you will need more than smarts. The greatest leaders deliver quantifiable, real-world results for their team, their organisation, themselves. This endeavour is a life-long learning, yet there are some foundations you can fix into place now, to ensure your leadership endeavours truly deliver lasting results.

As you explore these fundamental elements of personal leadership, resilience and capability, reflect on your own experience of organisations, leaders or managers, and the people who create the results.

My three-stage approach helps me to forge better leadership in my life, at work, at home as a dad and a husband, and within myself. They will also help you shift your perspective, your behaviour, and your ability to create results together with those around you. Each stage is interrelated to create a powerful way of identifying successful aspects of the organisation, team, and strategy, whilst revealing challenges, often hidden in the complexity that spews forth when humans meet systems.

The three stages are:

- The Lenses of Organisational Power
- The Leadership Prism
- Navigating the Spectrum Map

THE LENSES OF ORGANISATIONAL POWER

Organisational power describes the effectiveness of an organisation in any marketplace, the marketplace being the field or environment in which the organisation chooses to operate. It recognises that capability does not simply consist of people and industry expertise alone, but it has interconnection across its people's needs (human capital), market intelligence and activity, and increasingly, the ethical and social considerations of the twenty-first century.

The key to navigating the complexity of any organisation is to hold up a lens that focuses your attention on a specific aspect of the organisational terrain. With a primary lens in place, you can then hold a secondary lens to achieve greater clarity and a third lens to establish a complete picture.

The three lenses are:

- Mission Lens
- Human Lens
- Accomplishment Lens

Every organisation operates through these three lenses—the specific balance, emphasis and priority given to each of them creates the organisation's ability to focus energy effectively (or otherwise).

Genuine leadership is essential to the organisation, and the Human Lens is often regarded as the most important, given leadership will or won't deliver without this lens. However, no team is disconnected from the organisation—effective teams need a sense of purpose and accomplishment to achieve their finest results. The method of employing all three lenses acts as a force amplifier, offering any organisation the potential to successfully leverage their full influence and power advantage in the market.

MISSION LENS

The Mission Lens focuses attention on the overarching thought-forms of the organisation. The ideals, protocols, values and reasoning behind the organisation are all visible in forensic detail when we hold up this lens. Starting with the vision that inspired inception of the organisation through to its ethics, policies, social impression, brand narrative and financial projections.

The Mission Lens reveals the architecture of the organisation in terms of Why. Why do we do what we do? But also in the How. How do we do what we do?

Ethics and Values
Environmental
Leadership
Social Impression
Governance
Vision
Market Need
Brand Narrative
Finances/Budgets
Audience/Clients

HUMAN LENS

The Human Lens hones attention upon the people within the organisation—the human capital. From ensuring each person has the necessary skills and opportunities to learn emerging skillsets, through the team capacity and performance, this lens highlights every human interaction, activity, and outcome within the organisation. When you see the organisation from the perspective of this lens, the human needs, strengths, limitations, results and challenges all become apparent—if you know how to translate what you see.

Whilst the other two lenses target other aspects of the organisation, any human element is revealed to us through this lens. Those policies, protocols, values of the mission—all created by humans for humans. Therefore, this lens is the Who. Who does what we do?

Talent
Capability
Team Capacity
Team Performance
Loyalty
Succession Planning
HR Responsibilities
Training
Mentoring
Disciplinary

ACCOMPLISHMENT LENS

Finally, the Accomplishment Lens unveils the doing of the organisation—the action that forms productivity and results. Here, we are seeking to understand not simply the activity, but also the need for reflection and awareness. Organisational agility and flexibility are up for scrutiny here, as well as how challenges are met. Responses to the market, to needs and adaptations, the activities of external parties, such as the media—all under the eye of this lens.

Accomplishment is not only in the results, but throughout the activities of the organisation—from awareness of all relevant factors from within or without. The instinct and the muscle that drives successful productivity, but also understands how it delivered those results and how to do it more effectively next time.

The Accomplishment lens is the What. What do we do?

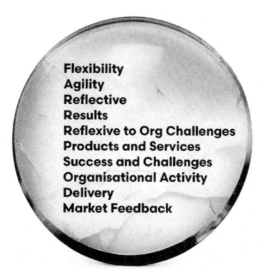

Flexibility
Agility
Reflective
Results
Reflexive to Org Challenges
Products and Services
Success and Challenges
Organisational Activity
Delivery
Market Feedback

Reflect on your own experience of organisations (in your career, as a member, volunteer or customer).

Which organisations excel in one lens but struggle with the others? What are the consequences? How did this impact you?

What difference does it make when all three lenses are brought together to act as a force multiplier, leveraging the organisation's influence, power and impact in the market?

Accomplishment Lens

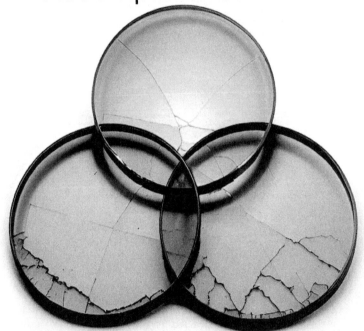

Human Lens   Mission Lens

THE LEADERSHIP PRISM

Combustion takes place when three essential elements are present at the same time. To start a fire, heat, fuel, and an oxidising agent or ignition source are necessary. When all are present and suitably combined a fire breaks out. Without any one of the critical elements, nothing.

A similar reality operates *within* any leader. When three vital elements are in place and active, the leader animates change. When one is missing, little to no progress is made. Historically, as we have seen, those elements consist of three intelligence forms. These are combined to engage inspiring leadership. Yet, we can take this a step further by adapting how we leverage those forms of intelligence.

Transforming cognitive intelligence by making it more more strategic in nature, we refine our approach for the organisational purpose. A Strategic Intelligence takes generalised smarts and thought with a laser-like precision that is forensic in nature.

An organisation does encompass emotional intelligence, however there is more to it than simply balancing emotions—here we need to harmonise all sorts of contrasting, even conflicting factors within the organisation. So, approaching our leadership with an understanding of how any one thing relates to every other thing can accelerate our ability to serve in exceptional ways.

The collective intelligence of teams, leaders, and followers is dynamic and capricious—in a constant state of movement and flux. Adapting intelligence to one that matches that dynamism of the organisation revels to us the kinetics all around us. Organisations move in ways that are comparable to a living organism or ecosystem. By employing Kinetic Intelligence, the leader can spot the movement, interact with it, respond to it and change it if necessary.

- Strategic Intelligence [SQ]
- Harmonic Intelligence [HQ]
- Kinetic Intelligence [KQ]

When combined within the leader, Strategic Intelligence (SQ), Kinetic Intelligence (KQ), and Harmonic Intelligence (HQ), transform the organisation's agenda into concrete, visible results. This fusion of SQ, KQ, and HQ, creates your overall Leadership Intelligence (LQ).

STRATEGIC INTELLIGENCE [SQ]

SQ

Sense—Vision
Principle—Thought
Modality—Creation
Primary Lens—Accomplishment Lens
Secondary Lens—Mission Lens
Polarity Lens—Destruction [A-]

Strategic Intelligence is the ability of the leader to focus upon important goals, outcomes or results and to design a robust strategy with the potential to realise these. It is viewed through the Accomplishment Lens, in combination with the Mission Lens. It is the creation of thought-based systems that achieve success, whilst remaining aligned with the needs/values of the organisation.

HARMONIC INTELLIGENCE [HQ]

Sense—Listening
Principle—Emotion
Modality—Interrelation
Primary Lens—Mission Lens
Secondary Lens—Human Lens
Polarity Lens—Chaos [M-]

HQ

Harmonic Intelligence is the leader's ability to bring out the very best of the team, enhancing their collective intelligence and capacity to work together effectively. This creates results that fulfil the strategic goals. Best translated through the Mission Lens, in combination with the Human Lens. Harmonic Intelligence weaves together the organisation's values, etc., with the people in the organisation and their needs.

KINETIC INTELLIGENCE [KQ]

KQ

Sense—Touch
Principle—Action
Modality—Momentum
Primary Lens—Human Lens
Secondary Lens—Accomplishment Lens
Polarity Lens—Inertia [H-]

Kinetic Intelligence is the leader's ability to build and maintain personal momentum, adapt to changing circumstances and take suitable action in healthy and sustainable ways. Felt in the most potent ways using the Human Lens, in combination with the Accomplishment Lens. Performance-driven.

Together these three intelligent forms can be arranged as a prism—one that refracts thought, activity and experience in different patterns; just as a prism splits and distributes light into a spectrum. The Leadership Prism is a device that receives our lens-focused beam of organisational power and splits it into an intelligent, valuable pattern or spectrum map.

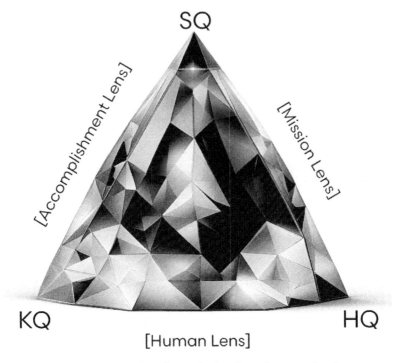

SQ

[Accomplishment Lens]

[Mission Lens]

KQ   **HQ**

[Human Lens]

Viewing an organisation through the three lenses, a leader engages the three intelligences in different ways to get the most from the resulting refraction map of the Prism.

- Mission Lens [**HQ**/SQ/KQ]
- Human Lens [**KQ**/HQ/SQ]
- Accomplishment Lens [**SQ**/KQ/HQ]

Here, we see the intelligences have a primary affinity with one of the lenses. A secondary affinity is also present, as is the need to balance all three lenses with all three intelligences of the prism. When this is done effectively, we see the organisation mapped through reflection. This is the Spectrum Map.

Reflect on your own experience of leaders (either of teams you've been involved with or your own leadership in different situations).

Which leaders were strong in only one or two of the intelligences of the Leadership Prism? What were the consequences of this imbalance or lack in overall LQ? How did this impact you, your colleagues, the projects?

What difference does it make when a genuine leader brings SQ, HQ and KQ together in their powerful Leadership Intelligence?

NAVIGATING THE SPECTRUM MAP

Effective leaders are not recognised by the loudness of their voices or dominating presence (unless you happen to be a Regimental Sergeant Major). They are recognised in the broad spectrum of results, traits, behaviour, relationships, vision, service, empowerment that follows them around.

When you inhabit your own high-performance leadership, you focus the Lenses of Organisational Power through your unique Leadership Prism to refract and reflect a rich spectrum of results, organisationally, relationally and personally. You can then use the spectrum to map a way of navigating through six distinct aspects of the organisation.

In this map, we not only quantify the organisational layers of Mission, Human and Accomplishment, to gauge how effective our use of the lenses is, but also we polarise aspects of the layers that are not beneficial—or even actively detrimental—to the organisation.

By calibrating your results through questions and analysis, you will see an emerging pattern of dynamics within the organisation that can be enhanced or modified through intelligent use of the lenses.

Our reflected layers are:

- Mission
- Human
- Accomplishment
- Destruction
- Inertia
- Chaos

When the three lenses and the prism are being used effectively, we will see the organisational success in Mission, Human and Accomplishment. However, if the Mission Lens highlights challenges, these will appear as Chaos. When the Human Lens reveals issues, these will fall into the Inertia position and finally, the Accomplishment Lens unveils truly Destructive dynamics within the organisation.

The method of adapting the results is grounded in the way we apply Intelligence, for example, when we peer through the Mission Lens and see its primary use with Harmonic Intelligence first and then Strategic Intelligence, we will see a Mission result. This is because when it comes to the organisational mission, we need to know the harmonics first, before deciding upon policy and protocol, etc.

When the Intelligence application is reversed (SQ then HQ), a

Chaos result is achieved, because the thought-based strategic approach does not consider the real-world harmonics of the situation, and so on.

The easiest way to understand the dynamics of the detrimental or successful results is to reflect on your own experience as a leader, as a member of an organisation or as a client of one.

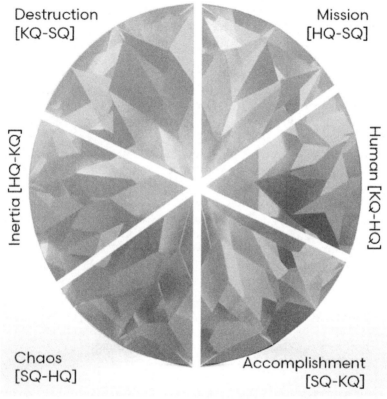

Destruction
[KQ-SQ]

Mission
[HQ-SQ]

Inertia [HQ-KQ]

Human [KQ-HQ]

Chaos
[SQ-HQ]

Accomplishment
[SQ-KQ]

Think about situations that are destructive in nature. Collect a couple of examples where the destructive elements are damaging the organisation. Can you identify where the moving parts (KQ) of the business (particularly teams and individuals) override, and are more dominant than the strategic elements (SQ)? How does this negate or damage the organisation's goals and strategy?

With the insight you now have, you can begin to address the challenge, reversing the emphasis—putting SQ first and allowing teams to be guided by this.

Think about situations where things simply got stuck, no progress was made, or things slowly slid backwards as everything else moved ahead. This is a result of when the harmonics of a business (HQ) are overriding the forward movement (KQ). When the ethics, values, principles, environmental concerns, etc. are focused on in a way that doesn't take into consideration the reality of the team and their capability.

For example, the team is doing their best, and then new require-ments are layered on top which they simply have no capacity to address, either because of lack of time, energy, skills, etc. How does this create inertia in the examples from your own experience?

Again, you can now begin to notice how it is possible to reverse the inertia by looking through the human lens to focus on the team first, the moving parts, and get them into a position where they are fit and able to deal with the harmonic needs.

Hopefully, you haven't had too many experiences of chaos in your organisational journey. But there are likely to be a few. Where were you? What were your roles? What was going on, who was involved, what were the consequences (individually, for teams, for the organisation)?

Where was the Strategic Intelligence (SQ) overriding the Har-monic Intelligence (HQ)? For example, the profit agenda and goal of quarterly increases in revenue meant the values of the business were compromised. Much of the greenwashing controversy can be identified in this dominance of the Strategic over the Harmonic.

Ultimately this behaviour causes chaos in the business or organisation as there is a conflict between mission and strategy. Understanding the need to reverse the dynamic, you can begin this journey by returning to the mission and work to make sure it determines the strategy, not the other way around.

Apply the insights you've created into these detrimental dy-namics to help you explore the success-creating dynamics on the right-hand side of the spectrum map.

LEADERSHIP EFFICACY

There is often a desire to state clearly or define the absolute characteristics of a leader. It is impossible to do this when trying to embrace a wide variety of cultural contexts, team and organi-sational challenges. What I *can state with absolute certainty* is the necessity of LQ when it comes to attaining that lofty position of being considered a leader. I have been fortunate to have led soldiers in operations and small teams in business, and I hope that my com-mitment to and dedicated use of these models has meant that the experience of those who have followed me has been positive.

I have been very aware of my behaviours (even when I have fallen short of the expectations that I place on myself), always attempting to be authentic. Who I am is how I lead. I am not a perfect example to follow, and indeed, neither is anyone for that matter. If there were a cookie-cutter version, then all leaders would look the same, each adopting this one persona rather than being themselves, and it would be like wearing the emperor's new clothes, see-through. Be authentic, be there, and be consistent. Leaders do not always start in a position of trust. It must be earned and valued. Trust takes time to build but can be lost overnight, so treasure it and nurture it, and you will reap the rewards of it through your followers.

The twenty-first century needs new leaders who are authentic, purpose-driven and who embody their LQ. Use your backstory to build your offering as a leader, along with your experiences, your vulnerabilities, and your authenticity. Do this, and you will attract followers. Do this, and you will become more effective with every step.

I wish you luck in this journey. It is at times scary, but it is also highly rewarding when you see and share the results that you can achieve.

Eight Rules
for Success

Nothing about life is linear apart from the direction of travel—none of us is getting any younger. We all experience highs and lows, fortune and misfortune, opportunities and threats, and plenty of unexpected challenges. Why do some people thrive against the odds while others can't succeed even when everything is going in their favour?

Leadership begins with the self, so it stands to reason that those who can manage themselves better and reach their goals are more likely to be able to lead others to help them achieve more. What do these highly successful people have in common? You may be expecting me to say intelligence, physical fitness, charm, charisma, or plenty of ideas, and they all have a part to play. What about the things we have more control over, our behaviours?

In this chapter, I have compiled a short list of some of the main rules or habits that the most successful, happy, and healthy people live by. I believe that if you take these on board and make them your own, you will also reap the benefits, and so will the people you care about.

1. DON'T HAVE TOO MANY RULES

Have you ever committed to a New Year's resolution (NYR) and failed in a miserable puddle of disappointment? I have, for sure. Why? Because I am the same as everyone else in the world, and by putting pressure on myself to act out of character and try to emulate behaviour that is out of my usual routine or range of habits, I set myself up to fail.

Habits keep us on a pathway, not out-of-the-ordinary commitments forcing us to swim in the treacle with countless other unfortunates, saying the same old crap, having just feasted over a holiday and feeling strangled with guilt. Small changes to our habits can bring about big changes in our outcomes.

The biggest issue with NYRs is that they often focus on external factors, such as appearance or material possessions, rather than internal factors, such as happiness or self-esteem. With research telling us that only an average of eight per cent of people stick to an NYR, the chances are that we have set ourselves up for failure and ultimately disappointment the moment we make one without treating the underlying reasons that led us to the resolution. It's a lose-lose. We've failed to address the real issue and failed to stick to the resolution. Set realistic internal goals and don't give them a title that associates them with failure, such as an NYR. Taking a daily stroll will do wonders for your mood and spirit but will probably help towards your fitness goals as well. You don't have to commit to a daily five-kilometre run!

Too many rules in our lives can have negative psychological effects. These self-imposed restrictions limit our sense of freedom, which can lead to feelings of frustration and stress. The knock-on effect is the opposite of what we wanted to achieve. Our motivation is sapped, creativity is dampened, and our sense of well-being is lowered.

Self-imposed rules only affect oneself, but once those rules become externalised, i.e., we try to impose them on others, we unleash a whole suite of other impacts. When we come up with rules for ourselves, it is not difficult to remember them even if we can't stick to them. Creating too many rules for others can lead to a sense of uncertainty as people in your organisation or those close to you may struggle to keep track of them. This can result in confusion and increased stress and erode the effectiveness of decision-making by working against the principles of the mission command concept.

Too many restrictions are likely to negatively affect you, your team, and your work. It is important to have some rules, but balance is the key. Allow freedoms within boundaries and create professional and personal safety and stability that allows growth all around you.

2. KEEP IT SIMPLE, STUPID—KISS

From a behavioural science perspective, seeking simplicity beyond complexity is critical because complexity can often lead to stress, confusion, and decreased motivation. When we are faced with complex situations or problems, our brains can become overwhelmed and struggle to find a solution. This can lead to feelings of anxiety and frustration, which can then negatively impact our behaviours and decision-making.

During my time as an Army infantry officer, we considered our approach to challenges in detail, producing complex plans initially, which we then looked at and distilled into a set of actions. We would practise those actions repeatedly as 'rehearsals'. As part of the planning process, we would consider as many what-if questions as imaginable to develop a range of 'actions on', or actions we would take if faced with otherwise unplanned events. You could think of them as if-then commands or routines—if A happens, we perform B—designed to ensure that nothing could knock us off track. By covering all bases, we'd still be in the simplicity zone if something unexpected occurred, even if that led to a more complex situation.

We worked on the assumption that no plan survives first contact. I have heard some people refer to this general principle as no plan survives contact, but if that were the case, what would be the point of planning? A plan that can't stand up to the test is no plan at all. Note that no plan survives first contact because, inevitably, at least one unexpected event will happen. A good plan will survive contact because when the curve ball comes in, your actions-on options are activated.

Complexity can obscure important information and hinder our ability to not only see but understand the bigger picture. For example, when we are faced with a complex task or problem, we may focus so much on the details that we miss the underlying patterns or principles; we don't see the wood for the trees. Seeking simplicity can help us to clarify our thinking and find the essential information we need to make effective decisions while keeping the big picture firmly at the forefront of our thoughts.

It's another one of those how to eat an elephant cases. When faced with complex situations, it can be tempting to try to tackle all the tasks at once; however, this can see our efforts spread too thin, which can lead to us missing critical elements. Seeking simplicity helps us identify the key success factors and focus our efforts on those things that will have the biggest impact.

Trust me; start with KISS! Seeking simplicity beyond complexity is critical from a behavioural science perspective because it can and, in my experience, does reduce stress, clarifies our thinking, helps us prioritise goals and tasks, and increases motivation. By embracing simplicity, we can improve our ability to make effective decisions and achieve our mission-orientated goals.

3. FIND THE PASSION FRUIT—NO PASSION, NO FRUIT

Passion is important for performance because it drives motivation and engagement. When we are passionate about something, we are more likely to put in the extra effort, persevere in the face of obstacles, and seek out new opportunities to improve. Passion also helps create and maintain a sense of purpose and meaning, which is the rocket fuel of high performance.

Furthermore, passion can enhance our creative and innovative abilities. Being passionate makes us more likely to think outside the box and come up with new and innovative solutions, but possibly even more importantly, we are less likely to be dissuaded from goals. Passion also helps us build our resilience as we are more likely to actively seek feedback and constructive criticism in an attempt to build our capabilities.

Passion stands the test of time. When I left Sierra Leone, I had a passionate desire to return to help others like the little boy whose hands had been cut off by one of the warring factions. It haunts me that humans are capable of this sort of horror. It is twenty years since I served in Sierra Leone, but that passion to return has never left me, and a little later in the book, I will share how I have turned that passion into action.

Without passion, you will be challenged on every front, so keep searching for the things you are passionate about. If you're not passionate about your current occupation, maybe it's time to consider a change. Passion is vital for optimal performance because it drives motivation and engagement, strives for continuous improvement, enhances creativity and innovation, and encourages collaboration and teamwork. By embracing our passions, we can achieve greater success and fulfilment throughout our lives!

4. TELL BRILLIANT STORIES

Storytelling is a powerful tool for communication because it appeals to people's emotions, imagination, and creativity. Stories can help listeners connect with the speaker on a personal level and can be used to illustrate a point or convey a message more engagingly. Effective communicators know how to use stories to make complex ideas easier to understand and remember. Think back to the last time you had to sit through a slide deck presentation at a meeting or training event. What can you remember? The chances are that you can't remember much of anything. Now see if you can recall a story a parent or guardian told you when you were a child or a film that held your attention for two hours and still makes you smile every time you think about it. See the difference?

A well-crafted story can evoke strong feelings in the audience and encourage action. Isn't that why young men feel so compelled to shadowbox around the room after watching any boxing movie? And isn't that why we all feel capable of anything after a feel-good film that invariably features heroes? Stories often have a universal appeal that transcends cultural and language barriers, making them an effective way to communicate with people from different backgrounds. Consider the importance of this in the modern world where digital technology allows us to connect to a global network of people from different backgrounds—culturally, geographically, and linguistically.

Telling stories not only enables speakers to showcase their unique personalities and engage with their audience in a way that is memorable and entertaining, but it also connects people on an emotional level. Connecting on an emotional level leaves a lasting impression, ensures our audience does not forget what we've told them, and can even trigger them to act.

BRING BORING STATISTICS TO LIFE

With practice, we can use stories to deliver information that would otherwise, frankly, be boring. Look for strong descriptive analogies that will help others to create mental pictures of your message, and be consistent with the construct.

For example, I was recently asked to show some data on the amount of time the junior talent community spent on learning across the year. To share this in hours would have been easy to do but even easier to forget, so after I had calculated the time spent for the whole community, I converted it into the distance we could have travelled in that time if we were moving at a steady velocity of 100 mph. That gave me 3,915,400 miles. By overlaying this distance over an image of the world on a slide, I could present the information in a far more interesting, visual, and quirky way. It turned out that the almost four million miles we could have travelled translated to 156 times around Earth.

A simple piece of data became a story, but more than that, it was thought-provoking because it drew on imagination. I was consistent with my construct because once I had decided to play with miles travelled instead of time spent, I stuck with the concept of distance.

I could have shown a rocket leaving orbit, passing the moon at the quarter-million-mile mark, and heading away from Earth.

It would have been handy if there were a few more planets within four million miles of the Earth but, sadly, the nearest is Venus at twenty-five million miles away. Still, with the distance we trav elled, we could have done eight return visits to the moon, and that's quite memorable.

The power of storytelling is undeniable, especially when you look at the trailblazers of our generation. Take J.K. Rowling and Oprah Winfrey, for example. They used their past struggles with poverty and their unwavering passion to change not only their own lives but also the lives of countless others.

STORIFYING A MESSAGE MAKES IT MORE VIVID

Imagine being passionate about extracting plastics from our oceans or a new technology that would allow the visually impaired to see more clearly. These are just a couple of excellent ideas that I've pulled from the top of my head, but as forward-thinking and noble as they sound, the most effective way of getting others to buy into them is through storytelling. Get the audience to imagine the oceans as they once were compared to how they are now and project their decline well into the future. Show them the visually impaired person who once struggled to cross a busy road smiling from ear to ear while watching a soccer match.

BRING YOUR AUDIENCE INTO THE ZONE

Key visionaries throughout history have told compelling stories to launch the most amazing ideas and change our world forever. Good stories create a speaker-listener neural coupling, which, in simple terms, means listeners' brains start to pulse to the same beat, and they all enter the same almost trance-like mental state. Tell great stories for great results.

5. BE KIND, BE KIND, AND BE KIND—SERVICE BEFORE SELF

Service before self is a leadership principle that I was taught in the Royal Military Academy Sandhurst, and have lived by, or at least tried to live by, all my life. At times, it's not easy, and, at times, it puts us in a place that challenges our very human instincts.

Walking to a nearby hotel where I was hosting an induction programme, I was crossing a busy street in Belfast when I noticed a group of youths. They were all scruffy, one of them appeared to be drunk, and I immediately jumped to conclusions and judged them for not being at work and causing a nuisance. Almost as soon as those thoughts had entered my mind, the seemingly drunk young man collapsed at the traffic light, and it wasn't just a fall; he was out cold on the pavement.

Walk on, Steve. Walk on, my inner voice was telling me, but I couldn't. I walked back across the road towards the group and carried out an initial assessment of the young man. Did he have any history of epilepsy or other condition that could have led to him losing consciousness like this? I asked the group. 'No, mister. Nothing.'

I placed a couple of my fingers against his carotid artery and felt a pulse, and I could tell he was breathing but it was shallow. He wasn't showing any signs of coming round. I called for an ambulance and placed the boy in the recovery position. As the person on the emergency line asked me probing questions about the casualty, and I relayed those questions to the rest of the group, I sensed some uneasiness. They appeared to be getting agitated, and I heard one of them say, 'Tell him.' It was time to act.

'What's the crack, lads? I don't know what's kicked off, and I don't care to ask your names, but it's better that you tell me whatever it is you know, or this boy could die.'

One of them spoke, and his words were like a heavy blanket folding on me: 'He's overdosed, mister. Heroin.' This changed the game.

I passed on this crucial update to the person on the end of the emergency line. They asked me if he had any naloxone, an opioid receptor antagonist that reverses the dangerous effects of opioids such as decreased breathing. The lads told me he had used the last of it, so I knew this wasn't his first overdose. How sad!

The ambulance crew arrived and took over; they and the person who took my call were all amazing. Why was this boy's life so cheap to him that he would throw it away and risk death for the possibility of a fleeting high? The medics would get him back on his feet, but it was a short-term solution, and I wondered what his other lows looked like.

I was disappointed in myself that I had hesitated before helping. This was somebody's son or brother, and he deserved the opportunity to build a new story for himself. Anyone can make a mistake, and when they do, you want someone there who can make sure that it is not terminal. I know that if it was my son, I would want someone to think service before self or to just be kind enough to do their very best and not walk on by. Who knows whether that young man has turned around his life or has fallen foul of the curse that is heroin addiction? Either way, I hope he is well and not just physically but in all aspects of his life. He deserves that at least.

Everyone does.

Being kind has a profound philosophical significance as it is a fundamental aspect of our humanity and helps us cultivate positive relationships with others. Kindness brings people together, fostering a sense of community, and promoting cooperation. It is also a form of empathy and compassion, allowing us to understand the perspectives and feelings of others, thereby reducing conflicts and promoting peace. Moreover, practising kindness can increase our happiness and well-being by creating positive feelings and reducing stress.

Kindness is not only beneficial to those who receive it, but it also causes a ripple effect that extends to others. It launches a virtuous cycle that benefits both the giver and the receiver, making the world a better place. Ultimately, kindness is a crucial aspect of our ethics and morality and represents the best qualities of human nature. Be kind with your time, your conversation, your money, your possessions, your heart and soul and give whatever you have when someone needs it. Don't hesitate! Someone might need it now.

6. DON'T GET YOUR KNICKERS IN A TWIST

One person's meat is another person's poison, and we all have a unique set of triggers that are almost guaranteed to piss us off or lead us to feel stressed. Some are highly organised but also highly strung. Others are more laid back but wish they had more time. With this in mind, I've put together a short list of tactics that help stop me from getting my knickers in a twist. Hopefully, they will also work for you or, at least, you can learn from them when it comes to dealing with your nemeses!

- If you don't have enough time, put your phone down or, God forbid, turn it off! There is a button for that.
- If you wake up with a good idea, get up, and write it down; you will have forgotten it by morning. I wrote 'Stand Down, Son' in eight minutes at 0038 hrs on 13 December 2022.
- Be friends when you leave the room; you might never come back.
- Walk barefoot on grass at least once a week; it connects us to our roots.
- If someone wants to borrow your book, gift it to them; it saves the disappointment when they don't return it.
- Tomorrow never comes; do it today.
- Failure is part of success; celebrate and learn from both.

- Surround yourself with the radiators in life, and avoid the drains.
- Stop listening to 'You're your own worst enemy' and start telling yourself 'You're your own best friend'; talk to yourself that way, and you will avoid many an argument.
- Don't be precious; life is too short (I need to tell myself this one, lots!).

7. LOVE FEROCIOUSLY, AND MAKE YOURSELF LOVEABLE.

Love is a vital human emotion that plays a significant role in our lives. Like kindness, it brings a sense of belonging and connectedness, promoting happiness and well-being. Love fosters healthy relationships, providing a sense of security, comfort, and support. It also has the power to heal, forgive, and bring people together, creating a more harmonious world.

Love also encourages growth and personal development by inspiring us to be better versions of ourselves and to reach our full potential. Love is a crucial ingredient in the formation of families, communities, and societies, and it is through love that we form meaningful bonds and connections with others. Love is not just an emotion, but a force that has the power to shape the world, making it a better place for all. No wonder so many songs have been written about it!

Love what you do, love the people you do it with and for, and love yourself (I know it is hard to swallow this one) because you cannot truly love anything else until you love yourself, and I do not mean in that destructive, self-centred way we see on social media or television; I mean in the way that you are doing your best with what you have and want the best for everyone around you, without envy, jealousy, judgement, and prejudice.

8. DREAM BIG

Dreaming big is a powerful tool for success in business and life as it provides a clear vision and direction for our goals and aspirations. We owe it to the world to dream big, and when we do, we set high standards for ourselves, which drives us to work harder and strive for excellence.

Having a big dream can also be a source of inspiration and motivation, keeping us focused in the face of challenges and obstacles. Dreaming big also encourages us to take risks and embrace new opportunities, leading to personal and professional growth.

Moreover, dreaming big has a contagious effect, inspiring others to aspire for something greater and pushing beyond traditional boundaries. Dreams that once seemed impossible can and have become reality. Dreams have changed the world. Humanity's greatest advances began in the minds of dreamers. I call them visionaries.

Dream big and act boldly. The world needs you and your dreams!

These are my eight rules for success based on what I have learnt and experienced. As you progress on your journey, embracing everything that happens with a growth mindset, you might discover other rules for success, or you may already have some. What counts is that we are striving to succeed systematically, noting the tactics that work, and avoiding the pitfalls that cause us to fail.

From the first chapter until now, I have been sharing stories with you to illustrate points or engage or provide context. In the example I provided about the young man who had overdosed on heroin, I said how much I hope his story changes and, notably, that he can write a better story for himself. Storytelling is one of the most powerful skills you can learn, so I have written a chapter to look at why stories are so powerful and how to become better at telling them.

Storytelling
—Painting Pictures That Change Mindsets

The gift of your past creates a vision for your future. Our past is the backstory that we can use to shape our future, and if we can focus on extracting the positives from the adversity we have experienced, we have an opportunity to create a story that connects emotionally, and that is a story that sticks to its audience.

A story doesn't have to have a beginning, a middle, and an end; most do, though, for a very good reason, which we will come to later. What all good stories do have in common is that they have emotion and connection. To tell a story well, we need to know what matters to the audience we are targeting and use that knowledge to ensure that we get the buy-in from them. If it is a business pitch, what part of the pitch does the client care about most? If it is a story to try to convince your team that it is not time to give up, get them to remember that thing that they all agreed to, that thing that matters most to them, that thing that will trigger a call to action.

The Army called out for me, and I answered. It was my first professional love affair. I can still remember the ad in the newspaper as though it were yesterday. Yes, the newspaper! I know some will not quite believe that we once looked for job and career opportunities in a newspaper, but it was the 1980s, and that's how it was done back then.

I was fourteen and totally fixed on that ad. It offered me a way out of Northern Ireland, an avenue to go and express my whole self, free from the shackles of being saddled with one side or the other, Protestant or Catholic. I could see the opportunities for travel, sport, adventure, professional skills, and so much more. I waited very patiently for four years until I was able to join at eighteen, and I never looked back, not even a glance.

During those early weeks in basic training, when things were pretty tough, I was able to use my backstory as my motivation. No matter how difficult things got, I knew I was not going back and was determined to keep moving forwards, always. I remember the first weekend we were allowed to leave the barracks, and we all went to the local town, Richmond, in North Yorkshire. It was gorgeous. Everything about the situation was just perfect; the sun was shining, we had money in our pockets, and a beer in our hands. This was our first taste of freedom for a while, and we had access to the jukebox, which was full of listings, but one stood out. It was the Clash hit 'Should I Stay or Should I Go'. I knew the answer to that one. Stay! We rocked the evening away, and I continued to rock my career in the military.

The power of storytelling in learning has been recognised for millennia, and societies around the globe have used it as a tool for transmitting knowledge, values, and culture from one generation to another; however, only in recent decades has the scientific community begun to study the impact of storytelling on learning from a psychological perspective.

Today, it is well established that storytelling can have a significant impact on learning, especially in terms of memory and motivation. Interest and research behind the psychological mechanisms and power of storytelling in learning have risen in prominence, particularly in the world of business where the focus is on how to leverage the strength and power of stores for selling to potential clients.

THE ROLE OF EMOTION
IN LEARNING THROUGH STORYTELLING

Psychological research has shown that emotions play a crucial role in shaping our memories, with emotionally charged events being more likely to be remembered than those that are emotionally neutral. Furthermore, emotions can also influence the way we process information, with information that is associated with positive emotions being processed more effectively than information that is associated with negative emotions.

Storytelling is an excellent tool for evoking emotions in learners. Using character development, plot twists, and vivid descriptions, storytelling can transport learners into the story and make them feel as though they are part of it. The emotional connection can help learners to better understand and remember the information presented in the story.

For example, a study by Marzano and Pickering (1997) found

that students who learnt about historical events through story-telling were more likely to remember what they had been taught than those who learnt through traditional methods such as lectures or textbooks.

THE ROLE OF VISUALISATION
IN LEARNING THROUGH STORYTELLING

Another psychological mechanism behind the power of storytelling in learning is visualisation. Research has shown that visualisation can play a significant role in learning and memory, with information that is visualised being more likely to be remembered than information that is presented in a single dimension or mode of learning such as by reading or listening.

When we think about the stories that live in our memories, we can easily close our eyes and replay them as though we were experiencing them again. I only have to think about the lyrics from 'Should I Stay or Should I Go', and I am standing with my friends in a pub in Richmond; it's that vivid. The memory is so strong, I can work through the entire representational system in my head, bringing all the sensations associated with the experience back to life—seeing my friends, smelling and tasting the beer, the feeling of sticky carpet underfoot, and the sound of the music, the loud, deep bass, and the singing.

THE ROLE OF STORYTELLING
IN PROMOTING VISUALISATION

Storytelling can be an effective tool for promoting visualisation in learners. Including vivid descriptions encourages learners to create mental images of the events and the characters in the story. This visualisation can then be used as a memory aid, helping learners to remember the information presented in the story, form relationships with the characters, and even begin to emotionally take sides. We can make much more of an impact with storytelling by using the right language and prompts to facilitate visualisation.

THE ROLE OF ENGAGEMENT
IN LEARNING THROUGH STORYTELLING

Another psychological mechanism that makes storytelling such a powerful tool for learning is engagement, i.e., the degree to which the learner is actively involved in the learning process and invested in the outcomes. Research indicates that learning outcomes, or performance outcomes if we were looking at truly measurable business learning, are directly proportional to how involved learners are in the learning experience.

Performance outcomes differ from learning outcomes because they show us what someone has been able to do because of what they have learnt. We are looking at achievement rather than potential. The level of engagement is a strong predictor of the success of the learning experience, and those who are more stimulated are much more likely to remember what they have been taught during the session. Telling stories increases that sense of connection and interest and therefore improves learning and performance outcomes.

THE CORPORATE LEARNING CONUNDRUM

Corporate learning refers to the process of providing employees with the skills and knowledge they need to perform their jobs effectively. In today's fast-paced business world, corporate learning has become increasingly important as companies strive to stay ahead of the competition and remain relevant in the marketplace—relevant in the 'war on talent' and for their client base.

Given the demands of modern working life, always being available in this ever-increasingly connected world of work is having an impact on our burn rate. As we continue trying to cram more activities online and offline into a static amount of available waking hours, something has to give. Many are becoming burnt out. The challenge for businesses and, indeed, employees, is finding the time and energy to take part in traditional forms of corporate learning such as all-day training sessions or death by e-learning.

MICROLEARNING

The corporate learning paradigm needs to shift to one where shared stories and experiences are delivered in a manner that can be absorbed in bite-size chunks and utilised immediately. This approach ensures content is learnt deeply, permanently, and in a way that transforms the learner. Moreover, this paradigm delivers learning in a way that is far more aligned with modern living and less likely to contribute towards burnout.

Bite-size chunks or microlearning provide one part of the solution. By breaking down complex subjects into smaller, easily digestible pieces, corporate learning can be made more accessible, less intimidating, and less time-consuming for employees. By sharing a learning story in chunks, learners will remain interested and invested and will absorb more with every chapter or episode until the conclusion is reached.

WHAT HAPPENS
IF YOU DON'T TAKE THE BITE-SIZE APPROACH?

You don't have to take the bite-size approach, but here are five compelling reasons why you should.

1. IMPROVED ACCESSIBILITY

Bite-size chunks of learning can be delivered on a variety of devices and platforms, making it easy for employees to access the information they need at any time and place. This means that employees can learn on the go, during their commute or while on a break, without having to take time away from their workday to attend training sessions.

2. INCREASED ENGAGEMENT

Combined with the use of multimedia, gamification, and real-life scenarios, we can make learning more engaging and interactive by splitting it into bite-size chunks. This makes the learning experience more enjoyable and helps employees to retain the information they have learnt.

3. INCREASED MOTIVATION

Using bite-sized chunks of learning allows trainers to provide employees with immediate feedback on their progress, which lets them see the impact of their learning and drives their motivation to continue. This type of feedback can also help employees to identify areas where individuals or the cohort need further development, allowing them to focus their learning efforts on the skills they need to improve.

4. ENHANCED MEMORY RETENTION

Learning is more easily digestible and memorable when it is split into bite-sized chunks, helping employees to retain the information they have learnt for longer. This means that employees are more likely to use what they have learnt in the workplace, resulting in improved job performance.

5. IMPROVED FLEXIBILITY

Bite-size chunks of learning can be customised to meet the specific needs of each employee, allowing them to learn at their own pace and in a way that works best for them. This can help to improve the overall effectiveness of corporate learning, as employees are more likely to engage with the material when it is relevant to their role and learning style.

A PAINTING-BY-NUMBERS APPROACH

The bite-size approach is a powerful tool for companies looking to improve the effectiveness of their corporate learning programmes. By breaking down complex subjects into smaller, easily digestible pieces, corporate learning becomes more accessible, stimulating, and effective, helping employees to acquire the skills and knowledge they need to perform their jobs more effectively.

If you want to learn to paint, you might want to start with painting by numbers. Breaking things into bite-size chunks is usually the best way of approaching things, whether we are looking at learning, building up strength and fitness, or anything else that involves getting from one position to another. That's why one of my favourite questions is 'How do you eat an elephant?', and you know the answer to that one.

STORYTELLERS WHO CHANGED THE WORLD

Storytelling is an art form that has the power to captivate, inspire, and profoundly influence people. Throughout history, there have been many great storytellers who have used their talents to entertain, educate, and motivate people on a global scale. Three of the world's most dominant religions have their roots in the Old Testament. Biblical stories are rich and diverse and embody the principles and ethics that form the foundations of societies on every continent. Who hasn't heard of Adam and Eve, Noah, Moses, or Jesus? A lot of the philosophy, ethics, and faiths of the Indian subcontinent stem from the Upanishads and the Bhagavad Gita, which are also full of memorable stories.

More recently, four of the greatest storytellers of our time are Steve Jobs, Oprah Winfrey, J.K. Rowling, and George Lucas, and they told us stories that changed our worlds. Steve Jobs, the late co-founder of Apple, was a naturally gifted storyteller who had a unique ability to present complex technology in a simple and compelling way. Jobs was known for his captivating product presentations, where he would use storytelling to bring his ideas to life. He used his powers of persuasion to convince people to believe in his vision for the future, and his stories about Apple's products and services inspired millions of people to join him on his mission.

Oprah Winfrey is a media mogul, philanthropist, and one of the world's most influential people. She is known for her powerful storytelling skills, which have made her one of the most successful talk show hosts of all time. Her ability to connect with her audience and share her personal experiences has made her a trusted and beloved figure, and her stories have had a profound impact on millions of people from the USA to the Republic of China.

J.K. Rowling has courted controversy recently because of some of the opinions she has shared on Twitter, but whatever you think of her opinions, nothing can change the fact that she is the author of one of the best-selling book franchises of all time, the Harry Potter series. Her ability to craft captivating stories that appeal to both children and adults has made her one of the world's greatest storytellers. Her stories have enchanted readers and inspired a new generation of young writers. Rowling's storytelling skills have also helped to raise awareness about important social issues such as power and corruption, bullying, and abuse, and have had a lasting impact on popular culture.

George Lucas, the creator of the Star Wars franchise, is another great storyteller who has had a profound impact on popular culture. His ability to craft complex and exciting stories that captivate audiences of all ages has made him one of the most successful filmmakers of all time. The Star Wars franchise is rich in metaphors, such as the Force and the Jedi, and it has more than its fair share of heroes. It addresses themes that everyone can relate to, such as the battle between good and evil, and the story has inspired millions of people across several generations.

These four modern virtuosi in the art of storytelling understand how to craft captivating stories that emotionally connect with their audience. They have made a lasting impact on popular culture, arguably changing the world on many fronts including that of business. Jobs, Winfrey, Rowling and Lucas have inspired millions with their messages of hope, determination, and their stories, as well as the creative way they have delivered them, will be remembered and enjoyed for generations to come. They are responsible for the fairy tales of the twentieth and twenty-first centuries.

THE STORYTELLERS WHOM WE MEET

We've looked at some of the greatest storytellers of our time, and they have become household names because of their skills, but what about the people we meet who go on to become our personal storytellers because of the impact they make on us? I have been fortunate enough to meet some of these very influential people but none more so than a man called Steve Edge.

Steve was introduced to me by someone who simply said, 'You should meet this guy.' And it turns out that he is the most generous man I think I have ever met—generous with his time, money, emotions, love, and experiences. I called Steve at the earliest opportunity, and he agreed to meet me for dinner at the Tramshed, in London, which used to feature one of Damion Hurst's unusual works of art—a full-grown cow and cockerel in a large glass container! We had a splendid evening together, and the Tramshed was very much part of that story, so I was sad to hear from Steve recently that the Tramshed has closed.

That meal together led to Steve supporting some of the programmes that I delivered in Ireland and London. He has a lovely TED Talk that was inspirational for me, and he has done me the honour of presenting this talk to the audiences on my programmes, which he does with much aplomb! On a side note, when he reads this, Steve will be pissed with me because he likes the language to be simple, and he definitely won't consider *aplomb* as simple language. He is charming, disarming, and brilliant. Quite frankly, Steve Edge is a beautiful man who inspires me to be a better version of myself. He has changed worlds, made himself vulnerable and available, and to those who have the pleasure of knowing him, loveable. When you meet Steve, he will advise you to 'Dress for the party, and the party will come to you.' I will add that Steve *is* the party.

I recently had the pleasure to meet another outstanding individual who helped me to understand, build, and tell better stories. That person is Richard McCann of The iCan Academy, a man with a very interesting backstory that I won't ruin by dropping spoilers. Take my advice and hear his story first-hand when you attend his Influence Storytelling Retreat, as I did. He shares lots of valuable insights that will transform your abilities as a storyteller.

Richard has built a career by telling not only his story but other stories that help organisations and individuals grow at every level. Richard has demonstrated that stories can shift opinion, start movements, and make people's worlds better through emotional connectedness.

Neither Richard nor Steve has any idea that they have been mentioned in this book. Hopefully, it will be a pleasant surprise and not a cause of embarrassment!

SO, HOW DO YOU TELL YOUR STORY?
START WITH PASSION AND EMOTION

You may not, or at least not yet, have a story that is going to change the world, but you are very likely to have a story that can change your world or the world of someone close to you. The good news is that there is a structure that can help us build our story in a way that paves the journey from start to finish, we just need to add in the bits that grab attention on an emotional level.

STRUCTURE

In her famous Harvard commencement speech, J.K. Rowling shared her three-part storytelling structure: trigger event, transformation, and life lesson. While this works for some, others may prefer a different approach. I like to use context, situation, and solution. The key is to find a storytelling method that resonates with you and your audience, so go out and explore the possibilities! Let's take a closer look at context, situation, and solution.

CONTEXT

This is where we set the scene and build the picture. Steve Jobs used this in his almost legendary launch of the iPhone in 2007. The iPhone was not the first smartphone on the market, so he had to come up with something special to make a bang. He hit the challenge head-on by acknowledging that Apple hadn't got there first but then throwing the gauntlet. Jobs called out the other phones in the market as not being so smart and reframed the iPhone as an example of reinvention. Instead of chucking just another smartphone into the mix, Apple was launching a completely new paradigm, and we know how that went.

SITUATION

The situation is the heart of any good story. It's where the tension mounts, the drama unfolds, and the audience becomes invested in the characters and their goals. Think of your favourite movies or fairy tales, and the chances are, they all have a compelling situation or conflict at their core.

In the story of the iPhone, the situation was clear; other smartphones on the market were frustrating users with their tiny buttons. Apple saw an opportunity to change the game by creating a phone that people could interact with using the most natural pointer of all—their index fingers.

By framing the situation as a struggle, Apple drew its audience in emotionally. People recognised the disadvantages of using a clunky smartphone, and they wanted to root for any person, product or organisation that was determined to solve the problem (in this case, Apple).

Whether you're telling a story about a hero battling a villain or a company creating a revolutionary new product, spelling out the situation is key. Paint a vivid picture of the struggle, and watch as your audience becomes invested in the outcome.

SOLUTION

Every story needs a resolution—a satisfying ending that ties up all the loose ends and often brings the hero's journey to a close. In many stories, this involves the hero defeating the villain and saving the day. Having clearly called out the villains in the story, Jobs presented the solution, a revolutionary smartphone that featured a versatile screen that could function as a keyboard, video player, or text reader.

This is just one way of looking at story structure. Another is to consider the story arc.

THE STORY ARC

The story arc is a fundamental structure of storytelling that outlines the progression of a story from its beginning to its end. It typically consists of an introduction, a rising action, a climax, a falling action, and a resolution. This structure helps to create a sense of progression and suspense and is used by storytellers to hold the attention of their audience and keep them invested in the story.

You can think of the introduction as setting the scene of the story; where is it set, what's going on at the time, who are the main characters, and how do they relate to each other and the context of the situation. Once the setting is established, we are ready to throw some spanners in the works to create the conflicts and dynamics that will drive the purpose for the protagonist, and a plot is born. As this plot thickens, and the tension mounts, this rising action leads to the climax, which is the point when something has to give—the turning point—and so begins the falling action where things start clicking into place, matters get dealt with, and we head towards the story's resolution.

Story tropes are conventions or recurring themes that are often used in storytelling. They are familiar patterns and contain elements that are easily recognisable to audiences and help to create a sense of familiarity and comfort in a story. Some examples of common story tropes include the hero's journey (iPhone), the forbidden love story, and the 'fish out of water' story, which describes how someone has to work hard to adjust to new surroundings and learn to thrive. The trope of my story could be described as 'the fish escapes water', as I was determined to break free from the oppressive sectarian culture.

The use of story arcs and tropes is important in storytelling because they help to create a sense of coherence and structure. They provide a framework for the storyteller to build upon and help to ensure that the story is compelling and memorable. By using familiar story tropes, storytellers can tap into the collective cultural knowledge of their audience, which can help to create a deeper emotional connection with their audience and make the story more relatable. In a nutshell, the audience can focus more attention on the emotional content and deeper message than trying to figure out the plotline.

Story arcs and tropes also help to create a sense of progression, suspense, and emotional engagement. By understanding and incorporating these elements, storytellers can craft stories that are more compelling, memorable, and impactful. I teach at a corporate university in Brussels and one of the sessions that I deliver is on storytelling. The firm I work for, a global leader in its field, is very much committed to leveraging the power of storytelling, not just to sell work to our clients but to build trust and connectivity with our community and demonstrate purpose. I have even recently seen a new role created with the title, wait for it, Chief Storyteller. That is a job I have got to have at some point!

Storytellers are everywhere. You are bound to know someone, an everyday person, who can make a trip to the local supermarket sound epic. In their own unique way, such people inspire and motivate us, even if only to make something as mundane as buying groceries into a more exciting experience.

Tell your story, look for the emotional connection, and grow your impact and audience. You owe that to yourself, and the audience waiting to hear from you.

All Roads Lead
to Sierra Leone

'Fucking hell! The road has collapsed, Sir. Help! The four-tonner has slid off the road,' rang out my colour sergeant's voice over the radio. There was no mistaking the sense of urgency, perhaps even panic, in his voice. The fact that Colour Mac, a man with a very cool head and years of operational service under his belt was reporting back with that tone alone told me the men were in deep shit. The content of his message simply confirmed it.

We were travelling as a convoy into the rainforest in the Guma Dam area, above Freetown, in Sierra Leone, for a training exercise in jungle tactics. Being able to operate successfully in the jungle environment is critical if you are to win the security battle in Sierra Leone, as the country is rich in this kind of terrain. If you can put aside all knowledge of the horrors that have been perpetrated under their perennial green canopies, any one of these jungles could feature in a list of the world's most beautiful locations.

What followed from Colour Mac's harrowing radio call was the stuff of movies. We planned to take a group of indigenous soldiers into the inner sanctum of their country to learn how to defeat an enemy from within, but a disaster was now threatening that mission. Instead of training soldiers on jungle military tactics, we had wreckage and casualties to deal with on a hill track in Guma, in an area that was forbidden for civilian traffic.

Apart from the lights from our vehicles, it was pitch dark, hot, and humid. Don't forget that we were in a tropical area of West Africa. This was the thick of the bush, so knowing that we were probably not that far from venomous snakes, including the green mamba, puff adder, and black-necked spitting cobra, along with other fun-filled wildlife from brown widows and African huntsman spiders to scorpions and biting centipedes added to the sense of adventure.

I halted my vehicle, which was at the back of the convoy, ordered the men to debus (get out of the vehicles), and made my way to the front. The wet season was ending, and the road, or should I say track, had been severely weakened by the rains. It had collapsed under the weight of the 'four-tonner' Bedford, which had lost its traction, slid off the track, and rolled down a steep hill. Carnage!

Bodies were scattered like breadcrumbs tracing a clear trail to where the vehicle had been brought to rest by the large trunk of a solid tree. The screams of the injured, the fear on the faces of my men, and the smell of the fuel that had spilt from the vehicles enveloped me like a perfect sensory storm. The situation was perfectly terrible, and only the arrival of the Four Horsemen of the Apocalypse could have made things any more dreadful.

The words *shit* and *holy fuck* went through my mind, but there was no way I could let those thoughts be openly expressed. I needed to shake myself out of this moment and take control of the situation. Everyone was looking to me for the what next, so this was no time for looking out of my depth or showing undue hesitation. Whatever I was about to do or instruct others to do would be the difference between utter chaos and controlled recovery. There was no space for emotion. The situation demanded a transactional approach. I needed to put together a plan quickly and make sure everyone was task-focused if we were going to minimise the death toll.

It was time for OODA, which, thanks to my training, was second nature—observe, orientate, decide, act.

OBSERVE

As I observed the scene, three priorities instinctively stood out: prevent any further injuries (which would include protecting my team who were about to spend the next few hours putting themselves at risk while rescuing others), get the injured to safety and medical care, and recover the dead, in that order.

ORIENTATE

Having identified the priorities, I had to break them down into tasks: first aid, setting up communications to our HQ to call for medical help, getting the troops stood up (being alert and prepared, ready for action), establishing an incident control point, choosing a suitable rendezvous point (RV) for onward movement, and gathering up the uninjured and getting them stood up. While all that was going on, we'd have to keep our eyes open for further danger. Observation doesn't stop after an initial assessment because the situation can change, particularly in a rescue situation in the field.

DECIDE

The beauty of OODA is its simplicity. It's a common-sense approach but needs to be drilled because common sense can easily fly out the window in high-pressure situations where the stakes are high. We knew what needed to be done and what resources were available to us. I had to decide who would be responsible for the execution of the tasks, and who would support them.

ACT

A plan without action is hot air, and we had no time to lose, so we would have to act fast if we were to prevent further loss of life. Over the next four hours, we worked through this extreme situation on nothing more than adrenaline and instinct. My team were exemplary, and it is down to their heroics that we managed to contain the situation, but we still had plenty of trouble ahead.

DEALING WITH THE INJURED

In Sierra Leone at that time, there was no access to the kind of medical care that most people living in a developed nation would expect. We moved the seriously injured to a UN hospital facility, but it had limited capacity. Those whom we could triage and treat within our team were moved to a nearby military facility, an open room in a compound that civilians did not have access to.

Moving the injured was another challenge. The Bedford was our largest vehicle and that was now on its side, halfway down a steep hill. A smaller vehicle had led the convoy, and that couldn't be used because its path was blocked by the collapsed road. That left two vehicles, a medium-sized truck and my four-by-four. The truck was dispatched to find medical help, and mine was used for taking casualties later when I drove to the UN hospital. In the meantime, most of the injured had to be carried to the nearest public road, so we could flag down and commandeer civilian vehicles.

We recovered three dead that evening, including one of my instructional staff from Sierra Leone's Army. No officer wants to lose men. The whole ethos of the Army is to move as a team and get everyone across the line, so although I was not injured, I was hurting too—hurting for my men. We began the evacuation of the men to our base and radioed ahead to have food and water prepared for them.

Shock would soon kick in for many, I'd seen it before and knew what to expect, so we had to act fast. I trusted one of my colour sergeants to take care of the recovery operation, while I took some casualties and made my way to the UN hospital to check on the seriously injured.

On arrival at the hospital, I was introduced to the doctor, who took me on the rounds to see the men. The situation was dire, but at least they had access to treatment that only the UN facility could provide. The first soldier I saw had suffered extreme trauma. One of his hands was literally hanging off his arm by nothing more than some thin threads of flesh. We both knew it would have to come off, but he needed someone to help him with the decision. I held him and told him there was no possibility of saving it. It was painfully ironic, considering all the amputations I had seen in Sierra Leone at the height of the conflict, mostly to children.

SHOCK

I left the UN facility to go to those who were being treated by my team. I was an accomplished first aider, and my skills and experience would be needed there, especially as soon enough they would be facing the effects of shock. Well-trained and experienced soldiers are just as susceptible to shock as everyone else, and it is a life-threatening condition. If in doubt, treat for shock is a well-known rule of thumb for first aid because this common reaction is a killer. Common symptoms include a weak or rapid pulse, pale or clammy skin, shallow breathing, dizziness or confusion, nausea, and fainting.

The floor was littered with injured men and women, our doctor was overwhelmed, and my team were all fully deployed. I got straight to work. As I made my way round, helping or treating those who had not had attention or needed more, I came across one man who looked quite gravely injured. His head was so badly swollen that his face was significantly disfigured, but he looked up at me, and it was clear from the expression in his eyes that he recognised me.

'Sir, Major McNally. Am I going to die?' he asked. It hit me like a thunderbolt. I recognised his voice. It was Officer Cadet Senessay, a wonderful man, full of energy, and the sort of character who would see that his country never returned to the violence of the near past. More than ever before, I needed to dig deep into my resolve. These people looked up to me as their military leader, and they needed me as their friend in that dire time. For those few seconds, that cadet was the only person who existed, because he was in front of me and needed some reassurance.

'We're not gonna lose any more men, soldier, and that includes you. We'll start by bringing this swelling down, so you look more like your usual good-looking self. Sit tight.' Mental strength is everything in any first-aid situation, and those few words of comfort and support could make all the difference.

A TEAM TO BE PROUD OF

We worked through the night to prevent any further loss of life. The injured recovered over the next week or so, and we visited and took care of the families who had lost their loved ones. Remarkably, one week later, all the soldiers returned to training, such was their resolve. This level of determination is rare in my experience, but when the purpose is so clear and the end state is one of such immensity that it overcomes even the biggest challenges, you can achieve things that may otherwise seem impossible.

My team did me proud that evening. When it comes to making the impossible possible, they nailed it, and it is thanks to them that we delivered on our mission. Again, I am not suggesting that the work we did during our tour is the sole reason that Sierra Leone has not returned to violence since the day we passed off (a ceremonial event at the end of any military training programme) our three hundred officers and soldiers, but we contributed.

Even writing this now, two decades on, I can see the faces of the soldiers and feel the anguish in their faces on that night. More importantly, I see the joy from the celebrations on the day we passed them off from the parade square in front of their president. Perhaps some of them have progressed to the rank of major by now.

The Steve McNally who led such an important mission in Sierra Leone is not the same person who is writing this book. These *are* my experiences, for sure, and I am the evolved version of the young Major McNally who played a part in the rehabilitation of a country that had been ripped apart by civil war; however, the key word here is *evolved*. Life's not about standing still and stagnating.

One of the reasons I decided to write *When the Going Gets Tough* was to express an idea that has been germinating in my mind for years. That idea is the thread. What's the thread that links that wee boy who lost his dad to the one banging out these words on a keyboard, and more importantly, where's it going to take me next?

Well, first of all, you're possibly wondering how this working-class lad from Portadown came to be an officer, and how he ended up in Sierra Leone.

FROM PORTADOWN TO SIERRA LEONE

During my first tour in Germany, aside from having an absolute ball of a time with new friends and experiences, I was beginning to not just find my feet but establish a good life there. I was quickly understanding how to play the game and was building a reputation for myself as a reliable soldier. In those early years, I trained hard almost every day, and that got you noticed, but it also ensured I was very fit and strong.

As for my general progress, I was knocking it out of the park, achieving outstanding grades across the board, and that included paying close attention to details when it came to standards of dress. The Army is a stickler for detail. Whereas civilians say a healthy body means a healthy mind, I'm surprised high ranks in the military don't say a spotless uniform means a spotless mind. Personal administration, as the Army calls it, is drilled into every soldier from day one and for good reason. When you're operating in environments such as the rainforests of Sierra Leone, you have enough to contend with without making matters worse because of an infection or something else that could have been prevented with good hygiene. Personal administration brings order to situations that may feel chaotic; in the long run, that's good for morale.

STICK MAN STEVIE

I was not a bore, but we had time and no distractions, so I trained and Ironed during the week and partied at the weekends. As sad as it sounds, I became so good at ironing, I gained the nickname Stick Man Stevie. In the British Army, the stick man is the soldier who stands on the front row on parade. Their proper name is stick commander or stick leader because they carry a baton or ceremonial staff. Being the stick man is a coveted position, and he is invariably the best-dressed man on parade. I wasn't the official stick man, but my title was just as hard-earned, and it came with some perks.

One job that nobody ever wanted to be lumbered with was 24-hour guard duty, but it was one of those things that had to be done, an essential part of military life. Those who were on the rota for guard duty would first have to line up for a parade. Nine soldiers would show up, but the one who was the most smartly dressed would be stood down and returned to their quarters; no guard duty for them.

I became so proficient at kit prep that I was always the one to get stood down. Eventually, if other soldiers saw that I was on guard duty with them, they would not even try to be the most smartly dressed, and Stick Man Stevie was born.

ON COURSE FOR LEADERSHIP

I was on top of my game as a soldier, and this led to me being nominated to go on a six-week leadership course back in the UK. It was an amazing opportunity, and I grabbed it with both hands. The training was gruelling, as we were physically hammered three times a day, and then there were classroom sessions on top, which included having to prepare and deliver presentations to our tutors and peers. I was young and enthusiastic and absorbed everything I could like a sponge. Neither public speaking nor presentations came naturally to me. I believe that culturally, we, the Northern Irish, are a bit shy in that respect, but whatever the reason, I was in the right place to shake it off.

Once I'd completed the course and returned to my unit and the more sedate day-to-day, I became bored very quickly. My eyes were peeled for the next challenge, which I decided would be to apply for officer training. I had the basic GCSE requirements, just, but nothing else, well, other than my determination. It turned out that was enough because I made it to Sandhurst via the Potential Officers Development Course.

SOCIAL MOBILITY AT ITS BEST

Three months of preparations for officer selection followed, during which time I was introduced, along with around twenty other soldiers from working-class backgrounds, to the finer things—theatre, ballet, and opera. We also got to learn the art of speaking in public with a confidence that distinguished us from most civilians and ordinary soldiers. Thank you, the British Army, for one of the best experiences of my life! This was social mobility in its most effective form. This wee boy from Portadown with no father, no education, and no right to be here had made it here anyway because he made it his right and grabbed the goal by the scruff of the neck: *I am going because I am good enough, and I do not need anyone to tell me or try to get in my way unless it is to help me clear the way.* Coincidentally, the regiment that I would join after the Royal Military Academy Sandhurst (RMAS) was the Royal Irish Regiment, and their motto is *Faugh-a-Ballagh* or *Clear the Way*.

The royal military academy was both interesting and challenging for me, with lots of academic work to do alongside the more recognisable soldiering, only this time, I, along with my fellow officer cadets, was leading, not following. I had to work hard on the academic stuff and needed help from my peers, just as they did with the stuff I was good at—soldiering, ironing, kit prep and, of course, drill practice on the square, and there was a lot of that!

A PhD?

On reflection, I believe leaving school with only five basic GCSEs made me feel academically limited. The reality was different, however, and the only academic boundaries I had were in my head. I had easily passed the very rigorous selection, much of which is academic, but I lacked confidence academically nonetheless. This is just one of many indicators of a deeper sense that, due to my background, I didn't belong, a phenomenon you will have heard referred to as imposter syndrome. Even now, I still question myself, far less than I did, but it happens in professional environments. These are situations that I am more than ready for, but there's that feeling—*what the fuck am I doing here, and how on earth did this happen?*

That boil of insecurity about my academic abilities, fuelled by my previous underachievement, was not lanced until much later when I got my MBA at Queens. Once I had ticked that box, I wasn't quite sure what all the fuss was about, but at least I would never feel the need to avoid answering the 'Which university did you go to' question. I guess it was like an itch that needed my attention. Getting the MBA scratched the itch, and I felt liberated, literally—free from doubt, insecurity, or any sense of not belonging wherever I wanted to be.

I recently met with my course director from the MBA programme, Professor Mark Palmer. He is such a fascinating man with a life experience not unlike my own in many ways. We were so immersed in the conversation, we only paused to stop our coffees from going cold. Mid-flow, Mark brought up the topic of potential doctoral opportunities (PhD) and asked whether I would be interested in applying. I was surprised but only because of remnants of the shadow of my poor academic history still lurking in the back of my psyche and looking for an opportunity to put me in my place—*You, a PhD? Who are you trying to kid, Steve? Stay in your fucking lane.*

Thanks to my MBA and the fact that I now have people like Mark, one of the most intelligent people I have ever met, standing in my corner, I was able to crush any negative self-talk before it could even complete a sentence. If a smart and academically accomplished individual like Mark believes I would be suitable for a PhD, I'd rather listen to him than my insecurities. The level of research and writing required to obtain a PhD is challenging for anyone, but Mark sowed a seed. Let's see if it germinates once I have completed this book.

IN THE THICK OF IT

Much of my early career as an officer was spent learning my craft, mostly on operational tours, digging into a wide range of challenging environments with my men. For an introvert like me, the pressures of being surrounded by the soldiers under my command were enough for another book, and the most demanding part of that was having to be always on and always available. If you know anything about introverts, it should be that we recharge our batteries by spending time alone, preferably in a quiet place.

Leading on tours was exhausting. On the other side of the coin, I got to travel to extraordinary parts of the world and take part in missions that would have otherwise been beyond my imagination. These opportunities have given me a rich bank of stories and experiences to call upon and built my resilience to such a level that I feel no problem or challenge is beyond me. That's not to say I don't feel pressure; I do for sure, but I am better equipped to deal with it because I have so many reference points that allow me to put things into perspective. Often, my go-to frame is *Well, nobody is shooting at me.*—at least not bullets, but words maybe.

Thanks to my time in the military, I have been fortunate and honoured enough to work with and for some of the most inspirational men and women on this planet. These are people I have learnt from and admired, near and far depending on how close I was to them in the role I was holding at the time.

FIRST TOUR AS AN OFFICER

My first operational tour following graduation from RMAS was a deployment to Northern Ireland! Most soldiers relish the thought of being deployed in hot zones where their skills are required, but they expect them to be somewhere on the other side of the world or at least somewhere other than where they grew up. The idea of being sent home to Northern Ireland as a soldier felt somewhat surreal.

My deployment to Northern Ireland came twenty years after my dad's murder, and I was about to tour the very streets that ultimately claimed his life. I was conditioned to deal with everything tactically that would come my way, but the idea of being responsible for preventing the loss of property and life in the community that failed to protect my dad was a tough one to process, especially for a 26-year-old on his first tour as an officer. Talk about cognitive dissonance!

Once I was there, I just got stuck into the role, and everything turned out okay, but I had an unrelenting work ethic. This resulted in some good soldiering but occasionally caused trouble with my troops, who I pushed hard, sometimes too hard, and they would complain about my unyielding drive. I wasn't going to apologise for having such a strong work ethic, but I did learn to be more aware of the needs of the soldiers under my command, and that experience was enough to trigger my intrigue about the relevance and importance of EQ.

Although I was slightly more aware, I was still a bit of a taskmaster, and that earned me my second well-deserved military nickname, Serious Steve, but I had good grounds to be serious; I was in a very serious business. We weren't rehearsing for a show on Broadway! My men didn't know what drove me, but it was a determination not to become the reason someone, some other wee boy, had lost their dad as I had done.

THE CALLING

I can now say that all of my time serving as an officer, both on operations and in barracks, was an absolute privilege, one for which I am truly grateful. It was not until I went to Sierra Leone that I experienced a tour that impacted me so deeply, emotionally and physically, that I would be left with a lifelong feeling of joy, passion, disgust, and the desire to return in a different capacity. I didn't know what that different capacity would be for a long time, but I am starting to get more insight into it now. I feel as though I am being called to go back, and the pull is stronger even than the one that led to me coming back to my own little torn country.

Plenty of books have been written about Sierra Leone's civil war. Ishmael Beah's *A Long Way Gone: Memoirs of a Boy Soldier*, for example, tells the story of how he was forced to fight as a child soldier. The conflict has been covered in Hollywood movies such as *Lord of War* and *Blood Diamonds*, which starred A-listers Nicholas Cage and Leonardo Di Caprio. Documentaries have been produced, and many others have written extensively on the topic, so I won't do the same. I will, however, offer a little context on how this beautiful country came to become one of the poorest and most despicable examples of human destitution.

Until the civil war, this country, which is about the same size as Ireland with a smaller population than London, was a good place to live. It was stable, tolerant, and prosperous. With plenty of natural resources, it was a net exporter of foods such as rice and palm oil, but the country also has the world's third-largest reserve of diamonds. When the country nose-dived around 1990, it was these precious gems that fuelled and funded its twelve years of brutal civil war. The main warring factions were the succession of governments that attempted to rule from the country's capital, Freetown, and the Revolutionary United Front (RUF) aided by Liberia in return for diamonds.

The fighters were often high on drugs and alcohol, which may explain, not excuse, some of the atrocities perpetrated on the country's soldiers and civilians, for they were not the actions of normal human beings. One such incident, which was observed and reported by the charity Human Rights Watch, was the attack on Freetown that took place during planned elections in 1999.

According to the reports, civilians were gunned down in their houses, massacred in the streets, thrown from the upper floors of buildings, used as human shields, and burnt in their cars and houses. They had their limbs hacked off with machetes, eyes gouged out with knives, hands smashed with hammers, and bodies burnt with boiling water. Women and girls were systematically abused, and hundreds of children were abducted.

Life was cheap, and that was apparent to me on every level. When life is perceived to be cheap, death is even cheaper, and that's the most dangerous environment you could ever imagine. In my other tours of duty, there were rules of engagement and codes of conduct, but all parties knew what the risks were—serious injury, loss of liberty, or death. Not so in Sierra Leone where there were no boundaries to the depth of depravity that could be reached, and death was sometimes something to be wished for rather than feared.

MY TASTE OF PARADISE

After landing at Lungi airport, I jumped on an old Russian helicopter to take me across the peninsula to the camp at Freetown, where I was met by a familiar face, an officer I had worked with before. He showed me to the room that was to become my living quarters for the next seven months, and then we were off to Number Two beach. Those of a certain age would recognise Number Two as the idyllic setting for Bounty's 'Taste of Paradise' advertisements from the 1980s. How much had changed!

THE SCARS OF WAR

When I arrived at Number Two, it was anything but paradisical. Just a short hop from this beach was a rehabilitation centre for former child soldiers. Like the kids in the other nearby orphanages, these children bore terrible scars. The physical ones, which were easy to see, were horrific and debilitating, but what of the invisible ones, the emotional scars that were deeply engrained in the hearts and minds of these young children? Would they ever heal, and would any of these children ever feel normal again? Killing changes a human being forever, and if anyone who has had to take lives tells you otherwise, they are either lying or they are psychopaths. It is traumatic enough when someone dies as a consequence of an order being given or a trigger being squeezed, but the violence that took place in Sierra Leone was on another level—often up close and personal with knives, machetes and handguns. For children to have to witness that, let alone take part, fills me with an intense sense of sorrow.

I still carry a deep scar from the day I refused to help the boy with no hands who was tapping on the door of my Land Rover. It was the afternoon of a day that, all things considered, had otherwise been pleasant. I slowed down to stop at a junction, and the boy seized his opportunity to grab my attention. As I stared into his beautiful big eyes, he looked deeply into mine, pleading directly with my soul, reaching out to my humanity. No words were necessary. Those eyes said, 'Please, Sir. You can see what I am up against. Can you offer me a little help, something to eat, anything?' But all Serious Steve could see were the strict instructions not to give money to anyone begging: 'Help them help themselves, troops!' Pff! *Serious Steve takes his brief seriously*, so I had no intention of winding down the window to engage with this sweet wee boy. How could I be so cold?

I should have helped him, but I drove on, and I can never redo that moment, only replay it in my mind and feel utter shame and disgust for not doing what was right. If it makes any difference or redeems me in any way, I regretted my actions as soon as it was too late to change anything, and I vowed there and then to never not help again. Had I not made that promise, I am not sure I would have been able to continue with my duties as a soldier. Somehow, that decision helped me to reframe the situation in my mind and move on.

AN EYE FOR AN EYE, AND DEATH FOR PETTY CRIME

I committed all my energy to the training of the soldiers and officers and was determined to give them the best I had to offer while ensuring the same from my staff. I succeeded in that mission apart from one incident, involving one of my colour sergeants who had joined us from another African nation. Unbeknownst to all my staff, this soldier was staying behind at night and stealing from the trainees, and unfortunately for him, they were onto him and his number was up; they were planning on killing him. I did say that life was cheap! They would have buried him, and no one would ever have found him.

One of the junior members of my staff had got wind of the situation and came to my quarters to tell me. We had to act quickly because the other trainees were planning to murder him that night. I could understand why they felt so angry, but I couldn't allow him to be killed, not on my watch. Not only was it morally wrong, and I didn't want that on my conscience, but it would have destroyed our reputation as a unit and made it impossible for us to do what we needed to do.

Fortunately for the colour sergeant, I got to him before the others did and explained the situation. He was confined to his living quarters for five months. Living quarters! Better than a ditch in the bush, which is what I had been told the alternative would have been. I then had to calm the trainees down and assure them that the thief would never be back.

The fact that I acted swiftly not only saved a man's life but meant that we retained our integrity as a team and the trust of our trainees. Values are critically important and so too is how you respond to any compromise, either in yourself or your team. Forgiveness can be asked for and granted instantly, but trust, trust is earned through actions and reactions.

SOME GOOD KARMA

Before I left Sierra Leone, I was blessed with an opportunity to help. Passing a street vendor one day, I jumped out and bought his entire stock. That seemed the wisest way to help because it gave him a win commercially, and I could tell myself that since I had paid for the stock, I hadn't simply given charitably. That left me with a stall's worth of stuff that I didn't want or need, mainly candy. Just across the road from where I had stopped, there was a little school, and all the kids were playing outside for break time, immaculately dressed and loving life. You can probably guess what I did with the sweets; I took them over to the school, beckoned a teacher, and asked her to give them to the kids. What happened next will stay with me for the rest of my life.

As I was making my way to the Land Rover, the teacher called me back. She'd gathered all the children to the perimeter fence, and before I could say anything, she broke into song, and the children joined in. I couldn't understand the words they were singing, but I'm pretty sure it was a song of gratitude, and it was the sweetest sound I'd ever heard. Suddenly, without any warning, I burst into tears, and they flowed uncontrollably from somewhere deep. Was it joy, sorrow, pity, or just the release of all my emotions that had been building up during my time in the country? I will never know, but those tears poured out of me.

When the children finished singing, I gathered myself, thanked them, and left. I vowed to come back to Sierra Leone at some point as I did not think my journey had finished with my tour, and it hasn't.

HONOURING DESTINY

Last year, I met with Naomi Sesay, a charismatic lady who is full of life and passionate about bringing about change on an international level. She and I were working together on a programme for my current employer, but we connected instantly, and I discovered that Naomi has family in Sierra Leone and is planning an ambitious project there. That is something I'd like to be a part of.

In 2022, with the help of my friend David Meade and his team at Lightbulb Teams, I built one hundred and ten prosthetic hands for children under the age of ten. During our High Performing Teams training sessions, which David and I deliver together, we cover the issue of amputation academically and practically and delegates are tasked with building prosthetic hands, so we kill several birds with one stone; we give people a real-world problem to solve, raise awareness of the situation in Sierra Leone and beyond, and get to make a difference for maimed children by providing them with the prosthetic limbs we produce.

It has taken twenty years and many other experiences in between for me to finally start reigniting my connections with Sierra Leone, but as I have said in the title of this chapter, all roads lead there. That country is my destiny, and it feels as though it was always my destiny, even when I was a young boy grappling with the loss of my father and The Troubles of Northern Ireland. I didn't know it then, but perhaps whichever route I had taken, I would end up in the same place. Who knows?

Listen to your heart, go where it tells you to go, and do not think that time is the determiner; it is merely another part of the journey. I am looking forward to the work that I am yet to do in Sierra Leone. It is in a much better place than it was, its future is brighter than ever, and I want to be a part of bringing that about.

Being Dad
—Leadership in the Home

The early stages of my life were spent questing for a dad who was taken from me. What I have come to realise is that I was searching for an image, a manifestation of what I had conjured up in the absence of my dad. Who knows whether he would have been a good dad? Either way, he deserved the opportunity to try.

Looking back, I am grateful, not for the horrible circumstances that took my dad but for the fact that his absence put me on a path that has brought me to where I am today. I am a very proud dad and one that I hope lives up to the images and expectations that I formulated and hoped for in my dad.

It is time to end the myth of the complete or perfect dad or parent, the flawless person at the head of the family who has it all figured out. I demanded the faultless father figure each time a new man was introduced into our house and as expected, they failed. How could they succeed? I didn't just set the bar high; I put it into orbit where the air is so thin nobody can survive, and none did.

Now that I am a father, I have set those expectations for myself, only I have the advantage of knowing what they are and can measure my performance against them. The would-be father figures who came and went from my life as a child had no clue what I expected or wanted from them. Even with the added insight of setting expectations, when it comes to being a dad to my two boys, Ewan and Finn, I am still a work in progress and will inevitably make mistakes along the way, but I want them to feel free to tell me where I go wrong, so I can be better.

AN EVER-CHANGING WORLD

The world is a very different place from when I was a child, and it continues to move at pace. It will never move as slowly as it is now because it is getting faster every day. That is the landscape that we, as fathers (and mothers), must navigate, and we must do this for our children, so they are never alone when facing the challenges ahead of them.

The job of a dad in today's world is no longer to command and control but to cultivate growth and curiosity in their children, to equip them with all the tools and support needed to thrive in this super-fast, rapidly changing world. It is only when dads come to see themselves as incomplete, with strengths and weaknesses, needs and vulnerabilities, that they will be able to make up for their inevitable shortfalls in dispensing their duties as dads.

POWER DYNAMICS

Leadership has been becoming less hierarchical and more collaborative for decades now, and I was seeing this in the military as well as in business long before I became a father. This trend does not sit comfortably with all leaders, and it doesn't sit well with all parents either. It does with me, and I would advocate that while it may seem as though discipline is weakened as a result of reducing the power distance dynamics, it can have the opposite effect. Let's explore this idea.

People rebel against authority, especially when the threat of punishment is outweighed by the reward of mutiny and the freedoms associated with it. The opposite is that people are attracted to an environment of inclusion and equity, and being part of the process of building that construct is very powerful and can bring about high levels of discipline because everyone has come together to agree to those standards—collaboration over control. Distributed responsibility is more likely to be maintained to high standards than diktat. Put simply, people prefer to have a say than to be told what to do.

Have you ever, in your parenting journey, made up an answer or feigned confidence or just shut down a line of questioning? Yes, of course, you have! We all have done that. All we have achieved with this approach is to shut down curiosity. We do not know it all and should not pretend to do so. Curiosity is the gateway to courage, and we, as parents, have a responsibility to facilitate it, not shut it down.

In today's complex world, none of us can meet the know-it-all expectation, and those who try are on a path to exhaustion and potentially causing damage to their relationships. I have created some navigational tools to help me avoid having to feign confidence or, even worse, shut down a curious line of questioning:

- Situational awareness—constantly understanding our environment
- Relating—understanding, balancing and allyship
- Future-focused—what does the future look like and how do we turn visions into reality

SITUATIONAL AWARENESS

Having situational awareness as a parent means constantly being sensitive to and checking in with our children, staying abreast of their world and the changes that affect them. It means knowing what the ramifications are of actions they may take or have taken against them.

For example, the world of social media is a minefield for our children. We need to introduce them to this world and allow them to enter it as soon as possible but only when the time is right, and choosing that time will depend on multiple factors such as maturity and necessity. When that time comes, we must ensure they do not leave a trace that will negatively impact their lives long after they have posted an ill-thought-out statement or shared something too hastily.

RELATING

Relating is simply about building trust between parent and child. We have to balance advocacy with inquiry and cultivate an environment that is open, transparent and safe. This approach does come with the chance of conflict as our children may have difficulty relating to us or mistrust our motives, but that's where becoming effective relationship builders comes into play. Any good building starts with a strong foundation, and strong relationships are built on the foundations of inquiry and advocacy.

Inquiring means listening, really listening to understand, not answer. It means understanding viewpoints, thoughts, and feelings, all while suspending judgement. Tough? Yes, absolutely, it is. Good parenting is not easy. Being Dad is my favourite, most pressured, and most important job.

Advocacy is our opportunity to express our opinions, having listened and without aggression or defensiveness. If we continuously work towards finding the balance across inquiry and advocacy, we have a very real chance of being sought out by our children when they need help, compassion or a best friend who has been with them from the moment of conception; I, for one, want to be that person.

FUTURE-FOCUSED

Being future-focused can help us set goals and motivate and sustain the efforts needed to bring them about. Being future-focused involves creating compelling images of the future. If you can't see it, you can't be it, right? This is where we can use the power of storytelling to clearly articulate what that future might look like.

My youngest son is set on being a vet, and I often talk to him about travelling the world to help animals. I share with him stories of me and him running a vet practice together with a kennel attached (he is a dog lover). Then, the reality of what it takes to become a vet (in the UK at least) kicks in, and that prompts me to tell him of the challenges he will face, such as getting a place on a programme and the study that he will have to do to become a vet. Note that my advocacy is to make him aware of the commitment while supporting him fully, not to put him off the journey. I know how to leverage this goal to encourage him when his homework is proving to be tough, using a simple go-to story: 'Well, Son. You know what it takes to become a vet, and it starts now with your attitude to the work that is in front of you.' Harsh, I feel, but if he is to succeed, he has some big but not insurmountable challenges ahead. I so look forward to travelling with him, and if he still wants to, helping him to set up his vet practice and kennel.

YOU GROW WHAT YOU SOW

If you plant banana seeds, you get banana trees. Plant potatoes, and you get potatoes. When thinking and reflecting on the many experiences in my life, the good ones and the not-so-good ones, I have come to accept that they have all contributed to who I am today. Although I have had to do a fair bit of reframing to achieve it, I am comfortable in the skin I occupy. More than that, I am excited, thriving, and, importantly, learning to love this skin, not in a vain or egotistical way but in the sense that I am grateful for everything that is in my life, my wife, my lovely boys, and everything that has grown from what has been sown.

I have suffered, yes, properly suffered from imposter syndrome all my life. I struggled to talk about my dad having been murdered when I found out that he was not my biological father. I felt like an imposter son! That is not something for a little boy to have to carry, but I had to, and I can see now that I didn't do it very well.

It is only in the last few years that I have rekindled a relationship with my biological father. When I say rekindled, we dabbled briefly in my early twenties but I was not emotionally ready to deal with it, and I stopped all contact; it was not very emotionally intelligent on my behalf, especially as I ended things as abruptly and decisively as hanging up the phone, with no thought or consideration for what that may mean for him.

We are a work in progress, but he recently said to me that he was patient because he is my father and loved me all my life, even when the distance was far. I greatly respect that bravery from him, especially as I am not the easiest person to say those sorts of things to. It turns out we are quite similar, which spooks the life out of me, not that I am trying to open the nature-nurture debate here!

Now, on a personal level, although I have used the term in this book because it is one that many people are familiar with, I have banned the use of the phrase imposter syndrome and swapped it out for growth moment. That is, at any time I hear that voice trying to question how I have ended up in this position or with that opportunity, instead of feeding it with a power it doesn't deserve by calling it imposter syndrome, I seize the power that I have earned by seeing it for what it is, a growth moment.

Life puts us where we should and need to be, and how we perform at that moment is down to us, down to our experiences, and the investment we have from those who have sown us. In making this very bold statement, I am not saying that we cannot influence how this plays out. Of course, we can, and we can do that by investing in ourselves and designing our journey. We can never gain complete control, but we can design the journey by deciding where we want to get to and plotting a rough roadmap to take us there.

I have a vaultful of experiences and behaviours that I have been challenged with, and I have learnt to pivot each one of them to better inform me how to behave positively; how to be a dad who does not fail his children, does not fail to be present all the time even when he must be the disciplinarian, and how to ensure he is the constant good gardener creating the conditions for the best crop to grow.

PRIDE, JOY, GRATITUDE, AND RESPONSIBILITY

Being a father is a tremendous privilege that fills my heart with pride, joy, and gratefulness. I am grateful for many things, but the gift of fatherhood is at the top of the list. Starting our family brought plenty of challenges, but we overcame them. Most of those challenges were related to suitability; were we suitable gardeners for this very precious crop? Many can procreate, but providing the love, environment, and guidance to help children grow is a different matter.

I feel privileged because not everyone gets the chance to experience the unique bond that exists between a father and his child. When a man becomes a father, he embarks on a journey of love, dedication, and responsibility that will change his life forever. At least, it changed mine.

PRIDE

It is natural to feel proud as a mother or father, but we must also manage our pride so that it never blinds us to our behaviours or the behaviours of our children. Pride does not come before the fall if you do not allow it to trip you up! Remember, we grow what we sow. The pride of knowing that you have played an essential role in bringing a new life into the world and the pride of watching your child grow and develop into their own unique person is the highest reward this life can offer us. As a father, I have taken pride in being a positive role model and providing guidance to my boys. A father should be a provider, protector, and mentor who takes pride in shaping the future of his children. This requires us to hold ourselves accountable for our actions—always, not just when we think we are being watched!

A very good friend of mine (and a very caring and invested father), Steven Black, has been in the fitness and coaching industry for many years. The other day, he posted on social media that we have a responsibility as role models to set an example to others by engaging in healthy practices. Now, he has won accolades at a national level for his work in the field, so he could do what many others do and tell his clients that if they hire him, they will win competitions, but he takes a different approach. He tells clients that our children need us to set a constant good example, and a major part of that example is our attitude to health and how we manage to balance that with all the other things we need to consider in life.

We can choose the healthy path instead of self-gratification and overindulgence (apparently) without sacrifice, even if it feels as though we are giving things up, but we cannot choose self-gratification and indulgence without sacrifice. Choosing health and well-being means cutting out harmful things and avoiding chronic illness, poorer quality of life, and possibly an early exit from this world. People often talk about life span, but isn't it more important to consider our health span, especially as fathers (and mothers)? I want to be there for my children and to be healthy in all aspects of our relationship and for me, that means being physically fit.

JOY

Parenthood also comes with a fair amount of joy. My son has just walked in and told me about scoring two tries at his rugby practice, not something that would be that joyous for many, but I think it's tremendous as I know that he has struggled to find his fit when participating in team sports. I asked him to talk me through all the details, so I could live every minute of this little victory with him.

The joy of watching your child take their first steps, say their first words, and reach many other milestones is priceless. We can experience the same joy in sharing special moments with our children, creating memories through experiences that will last a lifetime, but we often miss the opportunity because of how our Western society has shaped parental roles. Often, dads have not been there for many of these experiences, but as society is evolving, I hope this is changing too because these experiences make us better. Being a father gives us the chance to make a positive impact on our children's lives—and the lives of others through their words and actions as they grow—and that is a powerful feeling and another source of joy.

GRATITUDE

I am very grateful for the opportunity to be a father and for all the blessings that come with it. We should be grateful for the love, laughter, and precious moments that we get to spend with our children. A father is also grateful for the opportunity to create a better future for their children and to make a positive difference in the world.

RESPONSIBILITY

Along with the many privileges of being a father comes even greater responsibility. We have a responsibility to provide for our children, both financially and emotionally, to protect them and keep them safe from harm. Fathers should instil values, morals, and ethics in their children, to help them become responsible, kind, and compassionate adults. We also have a responsibility to be present in our children's lives, to listen, support, and guide them through life's challenges, even when and possibly more so if the parental relationships have broken down.

THE EARLY STAGE WARNING

The transition to parenthood can be a challenging and emotional time for both parents, as they adjust to their new roles and responsibilities. One idea that can help explain the experiences of new fathers during this time is the maternal gatekeeping theory.

Maternal gatekeeping refers to how mothers can unintentionally limit fathers' involvement in parenting by controlling access to the child and being overly critical of fathers' parenting abilities. This can be especially true in the early postpartum period, when mothers may feel a strong desire to protect and nurture their new-born. This is nature, and it's not your fault, so it's good to be aware, dads!

For some new fathers, maternal gatekeeping can result in feelings of grief or loss as they struggle to maintain their relationship with their partner while also adjusting to their new role as a father. They may feel that their partner is more focused on the baby and less interested in maintaining intimacy or emotional connection with them.

It's important to note that these feelings are normal and understandable, and they don't necessarily mean that the relationship is in trouble or that you, the dad, are being excluded from parenting altogether. However, it's also important for both parents to communicate openly and honestly about their feelings and needs, and to work together to find a balance that works for them both. I did not do this well at the start and sunk myself into work instead of my responsibilities at home, convincing myself that my primary role was to provide. That was, on reflection, a cop-out on my behalf.

Some strategies that can help us dads feel more connected to our partner and baby during this time include but are not limited to (do not wait as long as I did to consider these):

- Actively seeking out opportunities to bond with the baby, such as through skin-to-skin contact or feeding
- Communicating openly and honestly with their partner about their feelings and needs, and working together to find a balance that works for everyone
- Being patient and understanding and recognising that the transition to parenthood is a process that takes time and effort for both partners

Being a father is a privilege that brings immense pride, joy, and gratefulness. It is also a significant responsibility that requires dedication, commitment, and love over a very long period. The

180

challenge never goes away. It just changes with time.

The role of a father is one of the most important responsibilities in the world, and the impact that a father has on their child's life is immeasurable. As a father, you must embrace the privilege and the responsibility that comes with it and strive to be the best father you can be. You will also have to get good at forgiving yourself for the inevitable mistakes along the way.

My experience of parenthood has been mixed, but I hope that it has positively helped shape me as a father, and I think, based on what my boys tell me, I am doing alright. It is my favourite job; I tell them that all the time and I really mean it. It feels like my purpose. It's my why, and my experiences have shaped my what and how.

I am the most privileged man on this earth to be Dad to my two amazing boys. My life, I give to you, Ewan and Finn. Love from Dad.

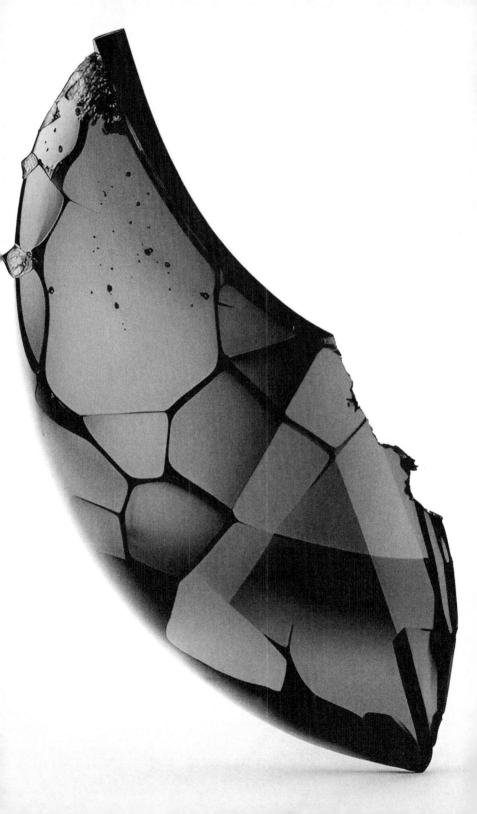

Reflections

The following chapter is a collection of letters written by people I have met, been inspired by or am very fortunate to be able to call friends. Some have asked to remain anonymous while others are happy to be mentioned.

If you have never tried this, I strongly recommend it. When you consider talking to your younger self, you cannot help but reflect on how far you have come. You may realise that you are making the same mistakes repeatedly. If that is the case, by bringing the issue to your attention, you have the chance to change it.

Nobody knows you as well as you do. At least, they shouldn't, so if they do, you need to fix that. Self-awareness is a superpower. Writing a letter to yourself is an excellent tool for improving self-awareness, but total honesty is necessary. Although some have shared their letters to their younger selves in these pages, you don't have to. Your letter is for you before anyone else. It is there to help you understand how you have grown and to recognise where there is room for further growth.

Letters to our children bring in a slightly different and powerful dynamic, prompting us to reflect on the impact of our actions on our loved ones. That should be painful because if you feel as though you have done it right, you are probably not being honest enough with yourself. I don't believe there is a parent on the planet who hasn't made mistakes. It goes with the territory. Acknowledging our strengths and weaknesses as parents gives us the chance to grow and improve. Again, it's not a confessional; no one else needs to see what you have written.

I am grateful to the people who have agreed to have their letters published. Every one of them resonates with me on some level, and I am sure they will resonate with you.

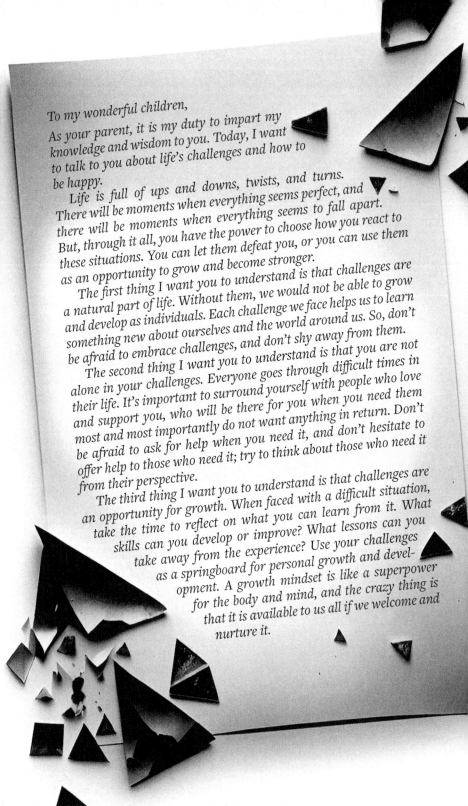

To my wonderful children,

As your parent, it is my duty to impart my knowledge and wisdom to you. Today, I want to talk to you about life's challenges and how to be happy.

Life is full of ups and downs, twists, and turns. There will be moments when everything seems perfect, and there will be moments when everything seems to fall apart. But, through it all, you have the power to choose how you react to these situations. You can let them defeat you, or you can use them as an opportunity to grow and become stronger.

The first thing I want you to understand is that challenges are a natural part of life. Without them, we would not be able to grow and develop as individuals. Each challenge we face helps us to learn something new about ourselves and the world around us. So, don't be afraid to embrace challenges, and don't shy away from them.

The second thing I want you to understand is that you are not alone in your challenges. Everyone goes through difficult times in their life. It's important to surround yourself with people who love and support you, who will be there for you when you need them most and most importantly do not want anything in return. Don't be afraid to ask for help when you need it, and don't hesitate to offer help to those who need it; try to think about those who need it from their perspective.

The third thing I want you to understand is that challenges are an opportunity for growth. When faced with a difficult situation, take the time to reflect on what you can learn from it. What skills can you develop or improve? What lessons can you take away from the experience? Use your challenges as a springboard for personal growth and development. A growth mindset is like a superpower for the body and mind, and the crazy thing is that it is available to us all if we welcome and nurture it.

Now, let's talk about happiness. Happiness is not something that can be achieved by material possessions or external circumstances. It is a state of mind, a way of being. True happiness comes from within, from a sense of inner peace and contentment.

The first step to finding happiness is to cultivate a positive mindset. Focus on the good things in your life, and don't dwell on the negative. Be grateful for what you have, and don't compare yourself to others. Remember, happiness is not about having more, it's about appreciating what you already have.

The second step to finding happiness is to prioritize your relationships. Spend time with the people you love, and invest in your relationships. Make an effort to connect with others on a deeper level, to really listen and understand them. These connections will bring you joy and a sense of purpose.

The third step to finding happiness is to take care of yourself. Self-care is crucial to your overall well-being. Make time for exercise, healthy eating, and getting enough sleep. Engage in activities that you enjoy, whether it's reading, painting, or playing sports. These activities will help to reduce stress and boost your mood.

The fourth step to finding happiness is to give back. Helping others can bring a sense of fulfilment and purpose to your life. Find ways to volunteer in your community or donate to charity. You will not only make a positive impact on the world around you, but you will also feel good about yourself.

In conclusion, life is full of challenges, but they are an opportunity for growth and personal development. Embrace these challenges and use them to become stronger and more resilient. Remember that happiness comes from within, and it is not dependent on external circumstances. Cultivate a positive mindset, prioritize your relationships, take care of yourself, and give back to others. These are the keys to a happy and fulfilling life.

I love you more than words can express, and I will always be here for you, no matter what challenges you may face.

With love,
Mom

Dear Younger Self,

As I write this letter, I am amazed at how far we have come in life. I want to share with you the lessons I have learnt along the way. These are the things that have made me the successful woman that I am today.

The first thing I want to tell you is that you are capable of achieving anything you set your mind to. Don't let anyone tell you that you can't do something because of your gender, your background, or any other reason. Believe in yourself and your abilities.

But, with that being said, don't be afraid to ask for help. You don't have to do everything on your own. Seek out mentors and advisers who can guide you along the way. And, in turn, be a mentor to others who may need your help.

The second thing I want to tell you is that failure is not the end. It's just a bump in the road. Don't be afraid to take risks and try new things. You may fail, but you will learn from your mistakes and become stronger because of them.

The third thing I want to tell you is that it's important to take care of yourself. Don't neglect your physical or mental health. Take the time to exercise, eat well, and get enough sleep. And, don't be afraid to seek help if you are struggling with your mental health.

The fourth thing I want to tell you is to surround yourself with positive and supportive people. Don't waste your time on people who bring you down or don't believe in you. Find people who inspire you, challenge you, and lift you.

The fifth and final thing I want to tell you is to always be learning. Never stop growing and developing as a person. Take courses, read books, attend conferences, and seek out new experiences. The world is always changing, and you need to keep up with it.

Now, let's talk about your career. You have big dreams, and I am happy to say that you will achieve them. But, it won't be easy. You will face many challenges along the way.

Here is some advice to help you navigate your career path:

Find your passion. You won't be happy or successful if you are doing something that you don't enjoy. Figure out what you are passionate about and pursue that.

Network. Your network is your net worth. Build relationships with people in your field and related fields. Attend events, join groups, and connect with people on social media.

Be proactive. Don't wait for opportunities to come to you. Seek them out. If you want a promotion or a new job, make it happen. Don't be afraid to ask for what you want.

Be flexible. Your career path may not be a straight line. Be open to new opportunities and be willing to take risks.

Don't be afraid to negotiate. Know your worth, and don't settle for less. Negotiate your salary, benefits, and working conditions.

Keep learning. Stay up-to-date with the latest trends and technologies in your field. Take courses, attend conferences, and read industry publications.

Take on challenges. Don't shy away from difficult projects or tasks. Embrace them and use them as an opportunity to learn and grow.

Give back. Help others who are just starting out in their careers. Mentor them, share your knowledge, and offer support.

In closing, I want to tell you that life is a journey. It's not about the destination; it's about the journey itself. Embrace the ups and downs, the successes and failures, the joys and sorrows. They are all part of the rich tapestry of life.

Remember that you are capable of achieving great things.

Reflection

They say hindsight is a wonderful thing and never more so than when we talk about life itself.

Do I look back at things I did and choices I made with regret? Of course, I do, but those actions, mistakes and moments that make me shudder when I think about them made me the man I am today. If we don't make mistakes, how can we learn?

My advice to my younger self would be around mindset rather than actions, although, yes, I wish I could go back in time and stop myself occasionally with a gentle nudge; 'Really, are you sure that's a good idea?'

My change in mindset would be around learning to live in the moment, being present and not elsewhere in my mind.

I have had some great opportunities throughout my life. Spending a year in Australia, even taking into account that I didn't bring all of me back. (In case you are unaware, this is where I lost my arm in a car accident) I think during this time, I was truly present and living in the moment, young and free.

After my accident, I worked as a scuba diving instructor on the Great Barrier Reef. Yes, I loved my job, but I am not sure I lived every wonderful moment just being present and dealing with what was given to me that day—weather, divers, sea conditions, and the creatures that decided to grace us with their presence.

Then the ultimate, twelve years as an international athlete. I believe sport can teach us so much, but one thing we don't do so well is that we are always focusing on the next competition, we spend very little time relishing in our achievements or most importantly forgetting the pressures of upcoming events and simply enjoying the ability to do the sport we love.

Now I am retired from sport and a grown-up in the real world, running my business and dad to three amazing children, but I still often find my mind switching from being with the family to thinking about work and business.

So once again, my advice to my younger self would be to practice being present and in the moment from a young age. It's a hard habit to break once it is ingrained in you. Life is an amazing journey, the highs, and the lows.

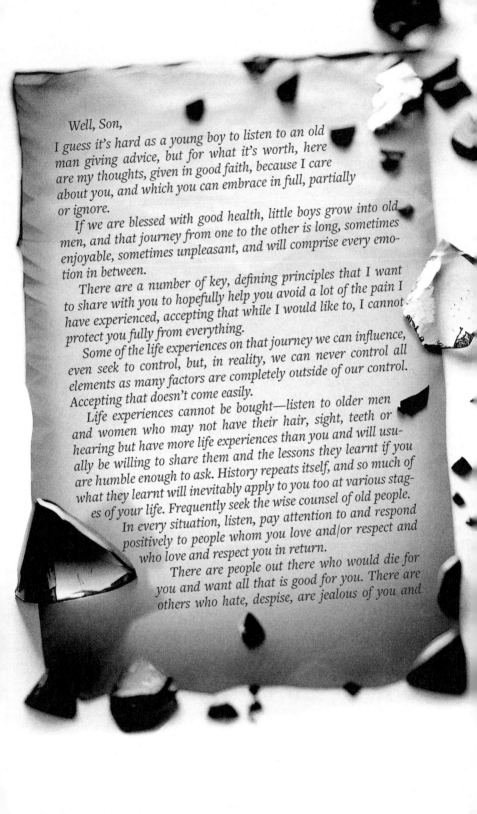

Well, Son,

I guess it's hard as a young boy to listen to an old man giving advice, but for what it's worth, here are my thoughts, given in good faith, because I care about you, and which you can embrace in full, partially or ignore.

If we are blessed with good health, little boys grow into old men, and that journey from one to the other is long, sometimes enjoyable, sometimes unpleasant, and will comprise every emotion in between.

There are a number of key, defining principles that I want to share with you to hopefully help you avoid a lot of the pain I have experienced, accepting that while I would like to, I cannot protect you fully from everything.

Some of the life experiences on that journey we can influence, even seek to control, but, in reality, we can never control all elements as many factors are completely outside of our control. Accepting that doesn't come easily.

Life experiences cannot be bought—listen to older men and women who may not have their hair, sight, teeth or hearing but have more life experiences than you and will usually be willing to share them and the lessons they learnt if you are humble enough to ask. History repeats itself, and so much of what they learnt will inevitably apply to you too at various stages of your life. Frequently seek the wise counsel of old people.

In every situation, listen, pay attention to and respond positively to people whom you love and/or respect and who love and respect you in return.

There are people out there who would die for you and want all that is good for you. There are others who hate, despise, are jealous of you and wish ill for you, and others who go with the flow and on a good day will back you and the next would let you down and undermine you. Seek discernment to know who falls into which camp!

Success comes at a price, and unless you are lucky, requires consistent hard work. There is nothing in this life that you cannot achieve if you put your mind to it. The price you may have to pay may be more than you are willing to pay, but there is nothing in your life that you cannot achieve. Ignore the many naysayers who will pooh-pooh your aspirations, and surround yourself with encouragers who also bring pragmatism and realism to support you—they are invaluable.

Success creates admiration and jealousy in equal measure, and if you are recognised as being successful, you will have a resentment target on your back. Discernment to know who feels which emotion is invaluable.

You cannot live as an island and as well as a circle of close, trusted friends, you will need a special lady to love, support, encourage and endorse you but also to provide a counterbalance and hand of caution where necessary. Choose your life partner wisely and look for evidence of her consistent goodness over past years from a range of people who know her and her family. Love her unwaveringly, honour and be faithful to her despite numerous female distractions and opportunities not to, be transparent with her in all matters but be sensitive and choose wisely your times to communicate sensitive matters—accept that you are not always right and a second perspective from someone you love and admire (most of the time!) and who loves and admires you in return (most of the time!) has a female perspective and often irritatingly accurate female intuition is invaluable.

Be brave and seize opportunities when they arise, after taking wise counsel from men and women you respect and who can speak with conviction from experience having walked a similar road to the one you are about to embark on or have insights that shed light on your proposed road.

Be honourable in ALL things. Never lie—reputation takes years to build but can be lost irrevocably overnight.

Be considerate of others and constantly seek opportunities to help and support others as a matter of course.

Be wary of others and do not run headlong into situations—always seek supporting evidence for perceptions.

Those who you least anticipate will let you down, and it hurts every time. Rise above it, retain your character and integrity and hold the moral high ground.

Forgive and do not hold grudges as you will suffer more than the perpetrator. Where appropriate, meet with the perpetrator and seek to understand why they behaved as they did. Share how their actions made you feel and shake their hand and tell them you forgive them even if every fibre in your body is resisting you doing so.

Religious faith is important and fundamental, but seek out real, relevant, applicable and relevant faith. There is a lot of religiosity that is simply emotional bubble and froth that is unhelpful, unreal and can be more constraining than liberating—seek to have a faith that lets you celebrate the reality of Jesus in your life daily.

If you are blessed with children and grandchildren, spend quality time with them as far as possible, accepting that young children need most when you are striving to build your career. It is a challenge that can defy you.

Accept that you will frequently make mistakes. Consistently learn from your mistakes and disappointments, but do not ever let them define you.

Be generous even when you are financially poor. Generosity is not defined just by money—it is an attitude of mind which entails giving time, care, simple hospitality, practical assistance and unwavering support. etc.

In summary, your starting point should be "Life is unfair, but you have been given life to make of it what you choose to—choose well in all elements and realise in full the potential your Creator saw in you when He made you and has given you to enable you to achieve His will and desire for you.

To my younger self,

Things are never perfect, just perfectly imper-
fect, and I still have mountains to climb, many of
which are the consequences of my, that is, your, actions,
so if you listen to what I have to say, you will create an
easier future.

First, forget whatever has already happened. Learn what
you need to learn from experiences and move on. Bearing
grudges will do you no favours, but don't surround yourself
with people who will stand in your way or hold you back.

Know that you can do pretty much whatever you want to
do. You are a creative soul with a flair for spotting details,
and you don't need any certificates or other forms of external
validation to assure you that you can. Trust me; if I told you
what is in store for you in the future, you wouldn't believe
me, and that's half of the problem—start believing now.

Be careful what you wish for. Your mind is deep, and
later in life, you learn how to use this to your advantage.
Don't wait until it has worked against you before figuring
out that you need to make your mind your best friend. Tell
it what it needs to hear—'I want, I can, and I will.' Imagine
the life you want to have, and believe it is possible.

Don't beat yourself up for making mistakes. Guilt
will do you no good at all. All that counts is what
you are going to do next. Don't be afraid of failure.
Winners die every day. As long as you are alive, you
are still winning.

Love yourself and know your worth. Until now, you
have spent most of your life making do and settling for
anyone who would accept you. The problem with

that needy approach is that you surround yourself with people who don't value or support you. You are special, you have value, and you have a place in this world. By the way, your father loved you; he was just too messed up most of the time to make you feel loved. Later in life, you will figure this out. Know it now.

Whatever you do, don't wait for things to happen. The world doesn't work that way. If you ever feel trapped, stuck in a rut, or on a losing streak, you probably are, and the only way it changes is when you change. If any of your employers ever tell you there are no bars on the windows, walk out immediately, and come back with a Thank You card, and a bottle of whisky; present them to your boss and resign on the same day. So you know, your future self never did this, and it probably isn't the best way to leave a job, but I am certain you will land on your feet if you do it.

Try to spend more time doing the things that make you happy. We both know what you're like, and almost everything you touch becomes a source of stress. It doesn't have to be that way. Learn a language because you enjoy the process, not because you must be fluent within three months.

You find peace in meditation and other spiritual pursuits. These work for you. Whenever you forget to practise, stress and unhappiness follow. Stay present, stay grounded, stay physically fit, and find as many outlets as possible for your creativity. That is the key to your sanity.

Finally, chocolate is great, but don't overdo it. Go easy on the sweet stuff. Your body doesn't thank you for it.

Chocolate is great, but don't overdo it. Wise words. There is a place for everything in moderation. Was it Aristotle who said that?

Now that my book-writing journey is complete and before you close this book and place it on the shelf, I'd like to share some final thoughts.

A Line in the Sand

MOMENTS

As the light draws in on the day
Has it disappointed or delighted?
Did you bathe in the simplicity beyond the complexity?
Did you fall in love with the problem
Or fall foul of the solution?

Yesterday will never be lived in again
Tomorrow is always just out of reach
Today, today is worthy of our reflections
Worthy of our preparation
For tomorrow we plan today
Look for and apply that extra one per cent

I am not what I have
I cannot control what others think of me
My achievements inform but do not define me
I am life, and life is me, I surrender
My intention is to connect and be connected

I have read many times that conclusions often disappoint. Not this one, not for me at least. In writing this book, I have written the book I needed to. I needed to exorcise some of my past and rebuild my backstory so that it supported my future story, not haunt me as it has at times. Our backstory is ours to shape and use to craft our future selves. Critically, we need to be comfortable with reflecting and reframing what has gone to help us build what is to come.

This book has been 50 years in the making, and it has taken me twenty-eight thousand, eight hundred minutes or four hundred and eighty hours to write about a journey that has seen many highs and lows along the way. It has reminded me, taught me, humbled me, made me cry, and made my wife cry, but more than anything, it has allowed me to rebuild my story into one that has made me more appreciative of the experiences I have had. They have all, in one way or another, contributed to the man I have become. I have shaken off the feelings of shame, the bouts of imposter syndrome, the anger, and, most importantly, the blame for the circumstances that were my childhood; maybe forgiveness is more appropriate than blame, certainly now at this point of the journey.

The story that I have shared with you in the previous fifteen chapters has, until now, been more like a collection of fragmented moments in my life, experiences, or memories, but now, now that I have stitched them together, they are very much my backstory and will inform my future story. I hope that you have been able to take something from my journey that will help you stitch together your story and tell it to the world. The world needs stories, big stories, and we all have them to tell.

My future story has to cover a lot of ground. I will be returning to Sierra Leone, and I will be bringing my story to life in the company of those who need to hear it most. The lessons I have learnt have waiting audiences, from small teams to large corporations to national bodies, waiting to apply the lessons rather than experiencing the pain of having to learn them.

FINAL WORDS

My final words are about taking responsibility. Knowledge of your backstory will allow you to engage with techniques, such as reframing, and will unleash the power to reshape your future story. Being present with a growth mindset will better inform the decisions you take and the subsequent impact you make. Self-compassion is good for our mental and physical health and provides a sense of safety that allows us to grow continually because we will make mistakes along the way to improvement. We can all, as I have, take our fates into our own hands! If you think that you are capable and want to transform, then you can. You must be prepared to take the steps, one of which is to be able to forgive, forgive yourself and others, and keep moving forward. Maintain the momentum, and, in no time at all, you will have formed new positive habits.

I am not saying what I have written is perfect, but these are my stories and lessons learnt in a life that turns out to have been a bit more eventful than the norm. They are my gift to you, and I hope that there is some interest or, indeed, benefit to you or someone who you know in what I have shared.

ENDNOTES

1 Do Employees Really Know What's Expected of Them? (2016) https://news.gallup.com/businessjournal/195803/ employees-really-know-expected.aspx?g_source=WW-WV7HP&g_medium=topic&g_campaign=tiles

2 Some excellent examples of impactful employee feedback can be found at https://officevibe.com/blog/ employee-feedback-examples

ABOUT MAJOR (RETD) STEVE McNALLY MBA

Steve McNally lost his father to terrorist action in Northern Ireland in 1979.

Faced with a life of social immobility, Steve chose to reject the inevitability of that future by escaping Northern Ireland and the limiting factors surrounding him.

Life in the British Army brought many challenges, but many more opportunities to grow and make a difference, sometimes at a national level. Following an excellent career in the military, which saw him serving in Northern Ireland, Germany, and Sierra Leone, Steve moved into the equally tough world of entrepreneurship.

After gaining an MBA from Belfast's prestigious Queen's University, Steve joined a global Big Four professional services company as a learning and talent lead.

Steve returned to his hometown of Portadown where he raises his family and continues his corporate leadership adventure.

Steve has won national awards and recognition for work done in the learning space. He describes himself as a raging introvert fighting every instinct in order to bring his personal leadership and resilience insights to those who need them most.

FIND OUT MORE ABOUT STEVE AND HIS MISSION TO NURTURE POWERFUL LEADERSHIP FOR ORGANISATIONS, INDIVIDUALS AND COMMUNITIES AT:

LinkedIn: www.linkedin.com/in/ stephen-mcnally-mba-cmi-fellow-1161b942/

Email: steve@realisingx.com

mPOWR TITLES

SPEAK PERFORMANCE
GES RAY

ISBN—9781907282874
For those afraid of speaking in front of a small team, groups of strangers or large crowds. How to be a confident, compelling and convincing speaker.

X CHANGE
LUCIA KNIGHT

ISBN—9781907282904
For those who are ready to torch their work treadmill, retire their boss, dump the ingrates, torment the passive-aggressives, escape the toxic office, get their fierce on and design the career that lets them live, love and laugh after 40.

LEGACY
MARTYN PENTECOST

ISBN—9781907282485
For those who wish to achieve immortality by leaving a profound legacy. Uncover the nature of lasting legacy and forge your mark through relationships, creativity, family and your work or business.

Printed in Great Britain
by Amazon

36223776R00119